WORDS FROM THE HEAVENS

DIVINE LINE ENTERPRISES
PHOENIX, ARIZONA

WORDS FROM THE HEAVENS

*Practical Messages of
Guidance, Love and Inspiration
from the Spiritual Realms,
with a Special Chapter on Death
and the Afterlife*

as received by
Eve Barbieri and Romayne de Kanter

DIVINE LINE ENTERPRISES
PHOENIX, ARIZONA

✢ WORDS FROM THE HEAVENS ✢

Practical Messages of Guidance, Love and Inspiration
from the Spiritual Realms,
with a Special Chapter on Death and the Afterlife

EDITING, TYPOGRAPHY & DESIGN BY SARA LYARA ESTES

DIVINE LINE ENTERPRISES
P.O. BOX 15177
PHOENIX, AZ 85060-5177
FAX (602) 977-2708

ISBN 0-9703404-0-0
Library of Congress Catalog Card Number 00-193305
Printed in USA on acid-free paper

FROM THE PUBLISHER

At the authors' request, the editing of this book was limited to spelling and grammatical correctness only. These messages remain in their pure Divine text. You are reading these messages exactly as the authors received them.

IN GRATITUDE

We wish to express our deep appreciation to Sara Lyara Estes, the editor/designer of this book. Sara came to us highly recommended, and has been a pleasure to work with. Her assistance and expertise have been invaluable to us.

Eve Barbieri
Romayne de Kanter

DEDICATION FROM EVE

I dedicate this book to God, our Creator; my little darlings Gina and Ryan James; my beloved husband Ryan; the archangels, all of God's angels, and the Ascended Masters —especially Saint Germain, who is my mentor and dear friend.

DEDICATION FROM ROMAYNE

I dedicate this book to my wonderful friend and husband Alex, to my family, and especially to Jesus and Mary, who are always and ever with me and fill my life with the most tender miracles.

ACKNOWLEDGMENTS

We acknowledge the *true* authors of this book—our Heavenly Father, The Lord Jesus Christ, Mother Mary, The Holy Spirit/ The Great White Brotherhood of God, Archangel Gabriel, Archangel Michael, Saint Germain of the Violet Ray, and Saint Francis of Assisi—and wish to express our deep gratitude for their unlimited love and patience.

This has been a work of joy, and it is our prayer that this book will find its way to all who love God and are seeking His truth.

We also wish to acknowledge all the elite forces of God for their presence and gifts of love during these writings.

Eve Barbieri
Romayne de Kanter

✢ CONTENTS ✢

✤ CONTENTS ✤

✛ CONTENTS ✛

INTRODUCING EVE BARBIERI
by Saint Germain

From November of 1998 until June of 1999, Eve suffered from intensely painful headaches. The three areas of immense pain were located in the middle of her forehead, the very top of her head, and at the base of her head where it joins her neck. Incidentally, these are three sacred areas of the physical head. Each headache would last for at least one full day and was debilitating. The headaches became increasingly more frequent over time. This was very unusual, since before this time it was a very rare occasion when Eve would suffer from a headache. She saw numerous doctors to no avail, except for a naturopathic doctor who (after doing a muscle test) told her the source of her headaches was spiritual. Eve then began a spiritual journey with Reiki.

After completing Reiki III Master, she went through a vortex tunnel of God's White Light. Three additional tunnels followed over the course of three weeks. These tunnels raised Eve's energy vibrations, her frequency. This enables her to hear and see (with clarity) messages and visions from the elite forces of God in the Divine spiritual realms. This is part of her life plan. She is under contract with God, our Heavenly Father, to be His messenger—to bring forth God's great wisdom, spiritual knowledge, and enlightenment. God's angels and the Ascended Masters, including me, Saint Germain, are here to assist Eve for the duration of her life's plan. She is an oracle for the elite forces of God. She is also a Reiki Master Teacher.

Eve resides in Phoenix, Arizona with her husband and their two young children. And—just a note—she no longer suffers from those headaches.

INTRODUCING ROMAYNE DE KANTER
by Jesus

Romayne de Kanter is an ancient soul, and her service to God dates back thousands of years. She is highly telepathic and has received messages from me and my mother, Mary, for years throughout this lifetime. She is one who exists on a very high vibration, therefore allowing light to enter her being and her soul. Romayne is also an ancient healer who works with my elite healing forces to bring harmony and peace to others. She works for the forces of my Command, and has for many eons. Romayne is one who shines the light of God to all she sees. She is a member of the Christ Light Command, where she is a loved and powerful advocate who serves the light of God, our Father. I am her mentor, and she is one of my very dear protégées. Romayne de Kanter is a Reiki Master Teacher, and she lives with her husband in northern Arizona.

FOREWORD / INTRODUCTION
by Jesus

Dear Reader,

Allow me to introduce myself and my co-authors of this book. I AM Jesus of Nazareth. My mother Mary, the Holy Spirit, (also known as the [Great White] Brotherhood), Archangel Gabriel, Archangel Michael, Saint Germain of the Violet Ray, Saint Francis of Assisi, and of course, God, our Heavenly Father, have used this book to impart some matters of truth concerning various topics. This is necessary because there is much in the way of mis-information being circulated in various books and (of course) the media, primarily television.

This mis-information, whether the bearer of the information is well-meaning or not, can cause many to believe in a lie. When a lie becomes part on one's belief system, it colors every part of their life. As an example, let us say you were told that God punishes and is just waiting for you to step out of line. If you hold this belief, it will affect how you pray and even whether you pray. You will live in constant fear, and if something unpleasant happens, you will feel that it is a punishment from God and not take responsibility for what you are creating in your life. You will look upon the misfortunes of others and judge them as a punishment for some great sin.

I have come again and again to bear witness to the truth. I speak the truth to every heart who will listen. Sad to say, too many of you trust what you read more than you trust your inner voice. Therefore, we have come to you in this manner, in book form, through these willing oracles who have placed themselves at our service, to get these messages of truth to you.

The universe is one of Divine Love and Divine Order. As I have told you, even the very hairs of your head are numbered. Every soul, indeed every particle of Creation is a part of God. So how, dear children, can a part of God ever be lost or forgotten? How can a part of God be condemned to burn in hell for eternity? This lie has caused many to suffer needless pain and anguish, as do all lies.

As belief in a lie colors all aspects of a person's life, so does truth. When you know a truth, it will affect you in a positive way. God's truth holds no fear of any kind. All concerns can be brought to God with confidence. Truth will open your eyes to beauty and wonders you have not seen. It brings joy and gladness with it—always. You will feel these things whenever you come upon Divine Truth. It is your spirit rejoicing. This is how you will know and recognize truth.

We have come to give you truth and guidance on some of the most serious problems in your world at this time. These conditions are of great concern to us. It is our hope and prayer that you will take these teachings to heart and pass them on. Every person can make a difference and change things for the better. Each person can pray, and this is most important. As you pray, also listen. It is in a still, small voice that God speaks to you, so listen closely. God answers each and every prayer. You will receive new insights, new understandings, and new ideas. God will always answer your prayers in the best possible way, for your highest good. This, dear ones, is truth.

Read this book with a prayerful attitude. Ask the Father to open your understanding and heal your soul. A truth is like a pearl of great price. Gather only true pearls and test them to be sure they are the real thing. Always ask, "Is this consistent with the Law of Love and Divine Order?" This is the test.

When trouble comes, get out of the mindset of punishment, and look instead for cause and effect and the lesson to be learned. Take responsibility for your choices and the part you played in the scenario. Do not blame God. There are automatic laws, such as gravity. Some of these automatic laws are not as well known or respected, but they are still laws and have consequences when ignored. A small child who does not understand the law of gravity is not immune from injury if they fall, nor did God punish this small child. Do you understand? The child will not ask, "Why did God punish me?" if the concept of punishment from God was not part of this child's belief system. Instead, the child will learn about the law of gravity and how it affects him, so he can avoid being hurt.

And so the knowledge we impart to you in the pages of this book is given to keep you from being hurt—physically, mentally, emotionally, and spiritually. We are with you as you read these pages and lessons, and will be happy to answer any questions you may have. Thank you for your interest in the truth. I, Jesus, speak for all of us who have shared in the writing of this book. May the truths you are about to learn bring you comfort and peace.

The Lord Jesus Christ,
received by Romayne de Kanter

Chapter 1

EMBODIMENTS, REALMS, AND DIMENSIONS

by
The Holy Spirit/The Great White Brotherhood of God

✤ EMBODIMENTS, REALMS, AND ✤ DIMENSIONS

Hello, and many love greetings. This is the Holy Spirit of God—the Great White Brotherhood of God. Tonight we wish to start by saying that we are a group of very highly evolved beings who serve God, the Holy Father, and *only* God, our Father. It is our great privilege to do so. We are the Council Members of Love and Light. Our name—The Great White Brotherhood of God—refers to the White Light of God. We are not of the white skin color. We are spirit beings, and we, the Great White Brotherhood of God—the Holy Spirit—always serve all of God's children in the name of God, the Father. We love and happily serve all the people of planet Earth—every skin color—black, white, brown, yellow, red, and any mixture of these fabulous skin colors. We love and serve every culture—every one. We thank you for allowing us to make that known.

EMBODIMENTS

Tonight we wish to give you some information on embodiments, realms, and dimensions. As you already know, you are a third-dimensional people who live on a third-dimensional planet. Your physical state—you as a human being—is third-dimensional. What this means is that you have three-dimensional embodiments that exist on this planet. Your mental body is one dimension. Your emotional body is another dimension. And your physical body is the other dimension. This makes up a third-dimensional being. This is not *just* who you are. You have other embodiments that exist in other dimensions. There is much more to you than you may think or know at this time. Your spirit body and etheric (heavenly) body are with you now, but will reside in the fourth dimension. Your Higher Self (or God-self) is with God in the Heavens, in the twelfth dimension. Your Higher Self, or God-self, is an aspect of you, a part of you, so to speak, that is *always* connected to you and *always* connected to God, the Father. Your God-self is the spark of life that came into being when you were created by God, and exists with God always. This is not to say your physical body or any of your other embodiments reside in the twelfth dimension. Presently, only your God-self, the higher part of your entire being, resides with God in this highly evolved place. So understand, beloved souls, you are always connected to God, our loving Father, even when you *think* you are not. It is only your thoughts of separation from God that keep you from connecting on a conscious level with God. All of God's glorious Creation is always connected to God. God is everywhere.

REALMS AND DIMENSIONS

We will now talk about some of the realms of the universe. A realm is different than a dimension. A realm is part of a dimension. A realm is known as a kingdom or an aspect of time and space. For example, your planet Earth has many kingdoms or realms which make up its three dimensions. There is the animal realm, or animal kingdom. There is the water realm, or water kingdom. There is the land realm, or land kingdom. There is the air realm, or atmospheric kingdom. There is the plant realm, or plant kingdom, to name a few. All of the realms of Earth are classified into three specific dimensions to make up your third-dimensional planet Earth. This marvelous planet

Earth is strong, very powerful, and rich in love and healing for all who dwell here. Planet Earth is a strong, living entity. However, the heavy toxins and pollutants that mankind is inflicting on planet Earth are causing a diminishing effect of the love and healing that is offered to all inhabitants of this mighty host—the planet Earth. That is a very brief summary of the realms of the third dimension.

Now we, The Holy Spirit, The Great White Brotherhood of God, will talk about the fourth dimension. In the fourth dimension, there exists the astral realm and the etheric realm. The astral realm consists of two levels or phases—the lower and the higher. The lower astral realm is a place of darkness. This lower level of the astral realm is where the dark spirits reside or live. This is a place of enormous density. All the very negative emotions that you may recognize thrive well in the lower astral plane. These dark spirits are here by choice; they have chosen a path away from God, the Father. The dark spirits have chosen by their own will to reject God's love and light and to try to destroy all they can by stealing power from some of the human beings of Earth. This is why it is so very important to pray twice daily for God's White Light of Protection, for the day and for the night. When you pray for God's White Light of Protection, you receive it instantly and absolutely *no harm* of any kind will come to you. The other level or phase of the astral realm or astral kingdom, is the higher astral kingdom. This is a place of much more enlightenment. The vibration of the higher astral realm is of a higher frequency than in the lower astral realm. In other words, the spirit beings who live in the higher astral realm or kingdom are more enlightened and carry much more light in their souls than the spirit beings of the lower astral realm.

The higher astral realm functions or vibrates on a "God, the Father, the Creator" level. The lower astral realm, simply said, is darkness.

After the astral realm or astral kingdom is the etheric realm. This is a place of great joy and happiness. The spirit beings who live in the etheric realm carry much light in their souls. They have a strong connection to God, the Father and wish to live much of their life serving His will. They allow God's love and light vibration to enter into their places of home and worship. The spirit beings of the etheric realm vibrate on a much higher frequency than the spirit beings of the astral realm. The spirit beings who live in the etheric realm have within their being tremendous compassion and love for all of God's infinite Creation, and they have great love for God, the Father. The etheric realm is a place of great beauty, as are all the realms of all dimensions in this infinite universe.

Next we will discuss the angelic realm. This is a place of great love and light, which shines on the planet Earth and all of this beautiful, vast universe. In the angelic realm is where the angels who serve the Lord God dwell. This angelic realm or kingdom is bountiful with great majestic beauty. The angelic realm is an active place that is very mystical. The archangels live here, as do the other angels that serve God, such as the guardian angels, the healing angels, the guidance angels, and the angels who visit all the places of this vast universe and anchor God's light by being the great carriers of God's all-powerful light, which embraces all of Creation. These are some of the angels who live in this glorious realm. These angels serve God, the Father by serving all of God's Creation. Angels do this with great joy and enthusiasm, for they delight in their service to the mighty

Creator of all, our God. The angelic realm exists in the fifth dimension. Now it is important to state that there are angels who exist and serve God in the higher dimensions, as well. Some of God's elite angels, as well as some of the archangels, dwell in the higher realms of the higher dimensions.

After the angelic realm, but also in the fifth dimension, is the Ascended Master realm or Ascended Master kingdom. This is a place of holy attainment. This realm is where a spirit being begins its journey of total oneness with God and Self-mastery. All the saints of planet Earth have ascended to this place and have begun their journey in the holy spiritual hierarchy. A saint is an Ascended Master. For example, Saint Germain is an Ascended Master, who has advanced into the highest spiritual hierarchy. However, not all Ascended Masters are saints. The Lord Jesus Christ is an Ascended Master, yet He is not a saint. The Lord Jesus is the Messiah, the savior and the Son of God.

Ascended Masters have attained total peace and hold tremendous light within their soul. In other words, the almighty love and light of God completely encompasses their entire soul. Ascended Masters and saints have found total harmony, as they are one with God, themselves, and all of God's Creation. They are very powerful beings who serve *only* the Throne of God. Ascended Masters are entrusted by God to perform many powerful miracles on planet Earth. The power of God, the Father is so vastly unlimited and almighty that it is many times unable to be understood by the minds of the human being. God, His angels, and the Ascended Masters create many miracles, both large and small, on planet Earth every day. As we have said, the Ascended Masters and saints, through spiritual evolvement, move up the hierarchy of God's light.

What this means, briefly, is that the Ascended Masters *graduate*, or *advance* to higher realms that are in the higher dimensions. The frequency in the fifth dimension and the higher dimensions vibrate on a very powerful accelerated level. One must live completely in oneness with God, the Father—with absolutely *no* ill thoughts of any kind and *no* negative, destructive emotions—in order to be able to live with the extremely high energies of these realms or kingdoms that exist in the fifth dimension and the higher dimensions of this universe. This is just a brief description in general terms of some of the embodiments, realms, and dimensions in this universe. God's ultimate Creation is vastly infinite. We, the Holy Spirit, the Great White Brotherhood, hope this gives you some thoughts on how there are many worlds in this beautiful, immense, universe created by God, our Loving Father. Our love is with you, and all that lives in your world, and all the worlds of this universe.

The Great White Brotherhood of God,
received by Eve Barbieri

Chapter 2

THE HUMAN AURA

by
Saint Germain and
The Holy Spirit/The Great White Brotherhood of God

✤ THE HUMAN AURA ✤

PART I:

INFORMATION ABOUT THE AURA
by Saint Germain

Many love greetings. This is Saint Germain.

I wish to reflect on as much as can be understood about the aura. Your aura is you. It is the part of you people feel when they meet you. Some people have auras that are strong and vibrant, and others have weak auras with tears and holes in them. The larger the aura, the stronger the aura is. The weaker the aura, the more weak-minded the person is. Let me reflect on what the aura is made up of.

An aura is made of protoplasmic energy. This energy is derived from the highest of all energy sources—God, the Father in Heaven and all Heavens. When a baby is born into this world, the aura is the strongest and most solid energy ever known to you as human beings. But as time progresses, the aura becomes damaged. Abuse given by parents weakens the child's aura, thereby allowing the immune system to weaken drastically. Child abuse is now so widespread that this is why there are so many more childhood illnesses than in the past. More sickness is allowed to come in through the rips and tears in the aura. If people, especially parents, gave the children of this world more love and concern, then most of the childhood illnesses would cease to exist. The aura can and does expel what we call love darts and hate darts. When one walks in peace and love given by God, the Father in Heaven, then every kind and loving thought, voice, and action expels love darts. The same is true for the opposite side. When there are arguments, fights of the physical nature, and mental and/or physical abuse done, then the aura expels from it these negative, damaging darts that cling to another person's energy field, their aura. These hatred darts burrow their way into the person's aura and affect the electro-magnetic system of the human body, thereby weakening the immune system and changing how they feel physically for the worse. However, when the love darts are expelled from a love being—a loving, kind person—the love darts not only attach themselves to the aura, but begin to repair it—to put patches of love on it, to mend it back together. And here is a gift that only the Heavenly Father can give—that is, the love darts keep multiplying. If they did not multiply in numbers, the human race would not be as you know it. In other words, much of the human race would cease to exist.

There is, for the most part, and always has been more chaos than there has been peace where you dwell. These love darts, as we so fondly call them, are actually made up of crystallized love fibers that come from God and they constantly repair the tears and rips that abuse has caused. That is why, when one does the will of God and does the charitable acts in the name of God, his/her good karma keeps becoming fulfilled. We call it the "Love Chain Reaction." The goodness of God flows and keeps flowing. I must say, though, the hatred darts, the nega-tive protoplasmic energy fibers (they are concentrated pieces in the form and shape of a small tube which is directed toward a human being or animal) do not have the power to multiply and keep on destroying. This energy does not come from God, the Heavenly Father. That negative energy comes from the fear, hatred, and prejudice of man. This energy is located only in the third dimension and the lower astral plane, which is in the fourth dimension. The love darts, however, beloved ones, are from the higher realms and we have an endless supply from God, our Father.

In closing, I wish to ask of you in the name of love and peace, to send out the love darts and to understand how damaging it is to send out negative energies to both you and the ones they are being directed to. Understand, the hatred darts leave holes in your own aura as well. But please always know that the love darts empower your aura in addition to helping the others.

I wish you God's love and peace always.

Saint Germain,
received by Eve Barbieri

PART 2

UNDERSTANDING THE AURA
by The Holy Spirit/The Great White Brotherhood of God

Greetings, beloved souls, from the Holy Spirit of God, known as The Great White Brotherhood. We feel it is necessary at this time to impart to you an understanding of some aspects of the human energy field.

The human energy field consists of several layers of energy that surround the physical body. Commonly known as the aura, this energy field contains the very essence of who you are. All your life experiences are recorded and contained in this field so they are not lost when the physical body dies. The physical body is necessary in order to function in the third dimension, but you are much more, in that you exist on an energy, or soul level, way beyond the physical you.

These subtle energy bodies can be sensed outside of the five physical senses, yet they affect the body in profound ways. For instance, when you think of someone you love deeply, your physical body responds to this emotion and generates a feeling of happiness and well-being, which stimulates certain chemical substances to be released into the bloodstream, which greatly benefit the human body.

On the opposite end, when you think of something unpleasant or traumatic, chemicals are also created and released into the bloodstream that are detrimental to the body, and when there is an overload of these chemicals, the body responds by getting sick in an effort to get rid of this chemical overload and rebalance itself.

Can you then see that the first cause is the thought? The Bible says, "As a man thinketh, so is he," and instructs you to think on "whatsoever is good, pure, true, and of good report." This is a prescription for life, for maintaining health, for healing of all diseases. You don't need a doctor to write this prescription (although they would do well in doing so), for your Creator has already written it for you in the Bible (Phil. 4:8), by the apostle Paul. To control your thoughts is to be a self-master, for all things begin with a thought, and all thoughts create. Therefore thoughts are things and often generate great momentum and seem to take on a life of their own, as in the case of long-standing cultural and religious feuds that progress toward all-out wars. This results from a thought combined with emotion, which becomes "energy in motion," likened to spiritual dynamite. In the third dimension it has a longer fuse so that when the fuse is lit, it takes somewhat longer for the explosion to appear. Not so in the spiritual realm, where all is lived mentally. Here the fuse is lit and the explosion is instantaneous, so you can see immediately the effects of your thoughts. Those who learn to control their thoughts now will have a much easier time of it when they return to spirit.

It is important to understand that whatever you put out in the form of thought and emotion will always return to you. It goes out like a magnetic boomerang, attracting other similar energies that are floating in the ethers, and then returns to you with a "bang." If you put out even a little love, you will receive more. If you put out a little hate, you get back even more, and attract more hate-filled people into your life. This is the law of attraction.

Everything counts and is recorded, no matter how small or insignificant it may seem to you—it truly is not. Like a stone thrown into a pond, there is always a "ripple effect." A good deed will multiply itself many times over. To fill your life with good deeds done with a loving heart is the best way to honor God and show gratitude for all your blessings. It is the highest form of prayer.

All beings have choice. You have the power over your life, your health, and all that surrounds you. It all begins with a thought. What is it that you want in your life? Do you want more love? Then send out thoughts of love to everyone and everything. Do you want more peace? Then send thoughts of peace. Do not complain. Pray instead. Bless instead. And watch the situation change for the better.

Take some time to be quiet at the end of your day, and examine the events that occurred. Bless that which needs blessing. Release that which needs releasing. See if you could have handled something differently and how, for the lesson will surely surface again and again until you get it right. Above all, see where you could have given more love. A word of encouragement, a touch, a smile, a compliment, a little note. Do not neglect these things. They cause the release of the good chemicals that keep you and your loved ones healthy and happy. If everyone sent more love notes, get-well cards would not be needed. Give the gift of appreciation, the gift of friendship, the gift of caring. For very little money, you can brighten someone's day and make a difference. Take care of one another and God will take care of you.

The Great White Brotherhood of God,
received by Romayne de Kanter

CHAPTER 3

FEAR

by
Archangel Michael

✤ FEAR ✤

Greetings, beloved, from the angelic realm. This is Archangel Michael coming to give you a lesson today on fear.

Fear is detrimental in that it takes all the joy out of life. It darkens all of your perspective and the way you view your life. What you fear, you come to hate eventually, for fear and hate walk hand in hand. Hate turns to violence, and then you have lost control. It all begins with fear.

I will give you another way of dealing with fear. Generally, what you fear is only something you do not understand, as in the case of meeting someone from a different race or culture. They are afraid of you and you are afraid of them, only because there are simply differences that are not understood. Approaching each other in love instead of fear prevents misunderstandings and opens the door to many interesting experiences. You can learn many things from each other and learn to appreciate your different ways and cultures.

To live your life from a perspective of love protects you and places you in the heart of the Father. He loves ALL His children. To love is to care. To care is to share. To share brings joy and many blessings. Do not neglect to do this, for this is the Father's will for His dear ones. True happiness is what everyone seeks—no matter who they are or where they live—and true happiness cannot exist in fear, only in love. Hate is poison. It poisons all that it touches and destroys the spirit. Banish hatred with love and prayer.

Now there are times when fear is justified, in that it comes to warn and protect you from dangerous situations. It is then a teacher to which you must give heed. To venture out to sea, for instance, in a violent storm would be a foolish and dangerous thing to do. In such cases fear is what saves you. This fear does not come to hatred and violence. This is how to tell the difference between fear that is wise and fear that is not. If you find yourself in a dangerous, life-threatening situation, then fear is normal. However, neglect not to call on us and God for help and protection. We are only a thought away, but you must ask for our assistance, as we cannot interfere with your choices.

If you live in love, if you listen to your inner wisdom, and if you ask for God to guide you, you can eliminate fear from your life entirely. NO THING can ever harm you, for by your own choice, you are in God's perfect care. This is a way of life—not a " sometime " thing when the mood strikes you, not a weekly thing when you go to church, but a daily, moment-to-moment state of mind in which all your daily functions are carried out. All things, all concerns, must be brought to God. He is not too busy for this—you are. Slow down and take whatever time you need to learn how to live in this manner and soon it will become the natural way of life for you with very little effort.

Like all new things, it takes much concentration and effort in the beginning, but after a while it becomes easy and familiar. Think of it as when you first learned to drive a car or started a new job. Well, dear ones, in a very real sense, you are starting a new way of life. But it is no more difficult than the others. Give at least as much effort and attention to it as you did to the others, and the payoff will be ever so much greater.

We who work in the Light of God will rejoice to assist you with this if you so desire. We can remind you and coach you through your day. We bless you for your efforts and offer you encouragement on your pathway of light.

Archangel Michael,
received by Romayne de Kanter

CHAPTER 4

ENERGY AND ITS EFFECTS

by
Saint Germain

✥ ENERGY AND ITS EFFECTS ✥

Hello and many greetings of joy from the Heavenly Realms. This is Saint Germain. At this time I wish to give important information on the subject of energy and its effects. Existing in your world is positive energy and negative energy. With this concept is how your world runs on electricity. However, I must say there is much, much more to energy than just electricity. Energy is every thought. Energy is every action. Energy is the life force. All human beings hold within their bodies enormous amounts of energy, which is continuously supplied by God, the Father. Depending on a person's lifestyle and mindset, he/she will hold either good energy within their being, or a person will hold energy that has been transformed into negative energy by the person's choices and kinship with darkness.

ENERGY AND WEATHER

The collective consciousness of mankind is a realm of very powerful energy. The collective consciousness of mankind changes global weather patterns, sometimes for the better and many times for the worse. The major upheavals of Mother Earth (such as earthquakes, volcanoes, hurricanes, etc.) are brought onto man due to the strong negative energy produced by the collective consciousness of mankind. Much of the hardships and catastrophes man has had to endure throughout time has been due to the negative energies from mankind's thoughts and actions that are released into the Earth's atmosphere. In addition, the Earth's very core is greatly affected by both negative and positive energy.

The negative energy from mankind stems from wars, hatred,

violence, lust, immoral sexual relations, greed and the abuse given to all of God's Creation on planet Earth. This negative collective mindset (consciousness) of mankind is greatly responsible for global warming, atmospheric changes, weather disasters, earthquakes, volcanoes and the heating of the Earth's core.

You see, beloved souls, when there is an area of the world where there is a tremendous amount of negative energy due to wars, hatred, and abuse from mankind, then this negative energy builds up and is not compatible with the Earth's life force energy. When this happens, the Earth is physically and chemically unbalanced. Eventually there must be a release, a change. And at most times it must be a drastic change in order to create a balancing effect which will cleanse and neutralize the negativity. This release or change may be in the form of a hurricane, flood, or earthquake. These phenomena will change and balance the energy of the Earth. Even the air and the soil's chemical compounds are changed after one of these events. This is done to bring the Earth into a sense of harmony.

You see, planet Earth is also a living entity, a very powerful living entity. You are a living entity and so is Mother Earth as she is your living host. Beloved souls, understand: energy exists everywhere, both positive (God energy) and negative, or dark energy. These energies also influence your every thought, your actions, and your everyday experiences. The dark energy wishes only to control the mind and body of the human being. By doing so, it feeds on your fear, which is energy. And energy is power. And of course, the opposite of this is true. The positive energy, the God light energy, wishes only to uplift and liberate you into a state of self-empowerment and true happiness. The God energy never controls the human mind at any time. God energy brings enlightenment, knowledge, and divine information to the human mind. All this is done for human beings' highest good. God is the almighty Source of positive energy. Positive energy is a *giving* energy. Negative energy is a *taking* energy.

THE ENERGY OF CITIES

Many cities and areas of various countries in your world are filled with chaotic, confusing signs, advertisements, and blinking lights. The human mind and brain is easily programmed by these various types of signs and lights. These fast-paced areas of your cities, with the flashing lights, the tall signs, and bold letter advertising changes your good energy to energy that is one of confusion. This chaotic and confusing energy disarranges the logic and sensibility of the human mind. This causes the stability of the conscious and subconscious mind to be constantly shaken and submissive. Many people have the feeling their mind is scattered, hence the expression "scatterbrain." This is an actual true and continuous state of mind for numerous people of your world.

ENERGY AND ENTERTAINMENT

Another very powerful influence on the human mind of all ages is television. The images from television are designed to flash from the screen in a precise manner in order to program the mind and brain. Most of this is geared to persuade you to spend your money on various items of pleasure. This is a negative programming method of the human mind.

Another major effect of negative energy is the viewing of violence on the entertainment screen, be it a television screen or movie screen. Allow me, Saint Germain, to give some enlightenment. When people watch these vicious acts and violence take place, even though they are "just acting" and are "not real," this absolutely has a profound effect on the human mind, brain, and body. Watching these negative acts portrayed, as well as doing these negative acts, actually changes the chemistry of the human brain and the human body. This instills fear into the human mindset, which changes the chemical makeup or composition of the person. The willingness to watch these harmful acts or to do these harmful acts of violence creates an energy of total fear and negativity in your auric field, in your being, and in your home.

Now, this is important to know and remember. When a person's aura (their energy field) is affected by fear, hatred, anger, and/or greed, and when there is negative energy in the home, then this negative energy becomes a target for the dark spirit beings who feed off this energy and magnify its destructive effects. Dark spirits can sense this negative energy and zero in on its location. As a magnet is attracted to metal, so are the dark spirit beings attracted to this fear-based energy. The dark spirit beings are drawn to this negative energy and all negative energy.

Negative energy—ALL negative energy from any source, such as television, movies, violence, abuse, drunkenness in the home and in the social places or by the hatred and prejudice in the hearts and minds of people—has a certain color associated with it. The color of negative energy is an ugly, murky grayish-green. This is not a color of beauty. This negative energy color, murky grayish-green, is not within the earthly color spectrum. This ugly grayish-green color would not be recognized by, or be known to, the human eye. The only way a human being would be able to see this negative energy color is if the person has their third-eye chakra open and completely activated, which allows the ability to see the colors of energy and other people's auras. Dark spirits can actually see this negative energy color and are drawn to it. Also, this murky grayish-green negative energy color is damaging to a person's aura by draining the auric field, thereby making the aura smaller.

Negative energy is not compatible in any way with the central nervous system and the immune system of the human body. Therefore, there is a tremendous amount of stress inflicted on the mind and on the human body when a person is subjected to this negative energy. Stress, generated by negative energy, produces harmful chemical toxins which accumulate in the body. This is one very strong cause of illness and disease in your society today. The cure for many *incurable diseases* is to completely avoid negative energy and not allow it into your being, your home, and into your lives.

Beloved souls, do not be your own worst enemy by inviting this negativity into your being. People will at times entertain and oblige darkness, which causes them much harm. This does not have to be, for God has given you free will and free choice. There are also many other choices that will bring health and happiness to you, and these choices are available and offered to you every day. For example, there are other television shows that will delight and entertain people of all ages. There are some shows on television that are pleasing, humorous, and educational, and that are not of a chaotic or violent content. There are movies in the theatres that are romantic and funny and uplifting. To watch these films would be a far better choice for the overall health of your body, spirit, and soul.

And another way to avoid negative energy is to stay away from the nightclubs and taverns where alcohol and drugs are so prevalent. One of the most detrimental places to be is in the nightclubs where people throw themselves into one another while listening to very loud "heavy metal" music (as it is termed). Any music that is termed "heavy" is not healthy. This music is very damaging to the mind and body. Understand, beloved souls, *music is energy*. Music is made up of a sequence of certain tones. All musical tones have very profound effects on the emotional, mental, physical and spiritual embodiments. These musical tones are either positive or negative in their effects. The way to recognize the difference between positive musical tones and negative musical tones is by how you feel while listening to the music.

Positive musical tones will put your mind and body at ease. You will feel peaceful and tranquil. Positive music tones relieve stress and bring harmony and balance to the electromagnetic system. They also promote healthy cell generation, which enhances the immune system of the human body. Sometimes when you listen to positive musical tones, you will feel inspired by divine influence. However, with positive musical tones you will always feel pure love.

The opposite of this is true for negative musical tones. With negative musical tones, a person will feel negatively charged. A person's mind and body will build up with wicked excitement. This misguided and wrongful energy will increase, making the person feel very uncomfortable, very anxious. Because of a human defense mechanism, the person will need to release this pent-up negative energy. Understand, the lyrics in these songs are words of destruction and the mind has been consciously and subconsciously programmed to carry out this evil. At this point, if alcohol or drugs are consumed by the person, then this person has little or no control over their thoughts and actions. This person has, by their own will and by their own wishes, allowed darkness to influence their mind and manipulate their actions. Negative music tones, along with drugs and excessive alcohol consumption, have a suppressing and subduing effect on the human immune system and central nervous system. This greatly reduces the health of the human being. Negative music tones, along with drugs and excessive alcohol consumption, disarrange the human mindset, diminishing all that is sensible and righteous. These also program and influence the mind to think in a confused and distorted manner.

As a result of the effects of negative energy, the part of the human mind and brain that holds within it love, compassion, respect for oneself and others, and the sense of decency is de-activated—*shut down.* This is the part of the mind and brain that is your strength, your power—your God-power. When negative energy shuts down or makes inactive this powerful part of your brain and mind, then the dark spirits can bring into your mindset fear, anger, hatred, greed, lust, and pandemonium. When people of Earth willfully bring negative energy into their being, they allow darkness to steal their power and put into action the dark spirits' destructive will.

POSITIVE ENERGY

There is, however, a glorious and wonderful other side to this— the positive energy. God, our loving Father is the true and only source of positive energy. The angels, saints, Ascended Masters, along with the very loving people of Earth are the rivers and waterways for love and positive energy to flow, bringing with it life-giving substance to the world and all its inhabitants.

Positive energy is uplifting, empowering, and continuously giving to all. Love is the foundation and source of all positive energy. This all-powerful God-given energy is the basis for all life. Positive energy is Divine love, and Divine love is the base for all Creation. Without positive energy existing and thriving in your world, all life would cease to exist on the planet Earth.

Prayers and meditation are acts that create powerful positive energy. Your faith in God is a form of positive energy. Charitable acts and acts of kindness will produce positive energy. Understanding, patience, tolerance, compassion, mercy and thoughtfulness are all components of positive energy. Positive energy is the most powerful energy source on your planet today—more powerful than a billion times the energy produced by all the nuclear power plants on Earth combined, and more. Pure positive energy has the absolute might and force to move mountains. The people of Earth have not yet advanced themselves spiritually enough to be able to utilize this God-given energy to its full potential. Positive energy has the power and authority to transmute and transform negative energy into love and peace energy. Positive energy has everlasting effects of goodness on the people and the lives it comes into contact with. Positive energy is all around you and is offered to you at every moment of every day and every night, if you so choose.

Positive energy also has colors associated with it. The colors of positive energy are vibrant and bright, and are absolutely a part of the color spectrum of Earth. The colors of positive energy will depend on which avenue it is derived from. For example, the energy color of divine love is a brilliant and radiant white light. The energy color of prayer to God, our loving Father, is white-gold. The energy color of meditation is gold, and the energy color of compassion is violet-pink. Positive energy colors are luminous, gleaming and cheerful, and forever give promise, hope, and encouragement to all. These radiant and glorious colors of positive energy enter into a person's soul, thereby increasing the amount of light held within his/her soul. The amount of light held within a being's soul determines the degree of spiritual evolvement. When people invite, by their own will, great amounts of positive energy into their life, the more luminous and powerful their soul will be. With great positive energy as a major part of your life, the stronger your connection to God and the brighter the golden path to heaven.

ENERGY AND FREQUENCY

At this time, I, Saint Germain, wish to inform you about the vibrations and frequency of energy. Understand beloved ones, energy is a vibration and it is the amount and pace of this vibration that is the frequency of energy. The frequency of energy is not perceived by the five human senses. However, the five human senses are affected by the *effects* of energy frequencies. Every embodiment of the human being—physical, mental, emotional, and spiritual—is continuously affected by the frequency of vibration. How this works is as follows: vibration is a series of cosmic radiant energy rays that are sent forth from the protoplasmic auric field. In other words, your energy field, your aura, sends out cosmic rays. This is energy. This energy vibration forms waves at different light speeds. The slower the light speed of vibration, the less light. The higher the light speed of vibration, the more light. Low vibration is slow, dense, and negative in its effects. High vibration is uplifting and giving of God's knowledge and is positive in its effects. This is the frequency of energy.

Understand, beloved souls, all spirit beings have an aura. All beings have an auric field, whether human, animal, or spirit. Your auric field stays with you for all eternity, as does the animal spirit's aura and the spirit being's aura. Everything that God created has an energy field, an aura, around it. This includes every mountain, every tree, every stone, every crystal, etc. Your aura is a major part of you, of who you really are. Your aura never dies, although it can be greatly weakened by the effects of negative energy. This is because negative energy vibrates on a very low frequency. This low frequency, these low vibration waves, shrinks a person's auric field, weakening it and tearing holes in it. This is detrimental to the health and well-being of humans. Negative energy robs people of their power.

Negative energy is positive energy transformed by darkness for the purpose of control and destruction. The dark side will trick people into believing that they (sometimes) feel strong and powerful when embracing negative energy. However, this is an absolute illusion, for the person's inner power, their true power, is controlled by darkness. Negative energy frequency shrinks the size of the human being's auric field, causing the aura to become small and compact. This has a destroying effect on the cells of the human body. The negative energy frequency causes the cells in the blood to turn against one another and to weaken. This causes unhealthy changes in the white blood cells which are the warriors against virus and infection in the body. It also causes some of the healthy cells in the body to become toxic and other cells to become frail and to rapidly decay. This is one major cause of cancer, organ failure, and disease in the people of the world.

Negative energy causes a major imbalance in the electromagnetic system of the body. This system is vital to a healthy and prosperous life. Also, negative energy causes stress and harm to the central nervous system and the immune system, and as I have said earlier in this chapter, negative energy is in no way compatible with these systems of the human body.

Negative energy frequency causes many of the body's DNA strands to diminish and lay dormant. These glorious chromosomal rods, your DNA, are the keys to unlocking many mysteries of the universe. DNA strands are the keys to unlocking and opening the doorway to your God-mind's knowledge of the universe. Negative energy—its frequency and all that it is—causes the physical body (which is a dimension) to rage war against itself. It causes an untimely withering of the human body's miraculous functions. Negative energy frequencies cause all the embodiments of the human being to progressively self-destruct. And the stronger the negative energy (the murky grayish-green color and the low vibration frequency), the more intense the effect.

The ways to protect yourself against this negative force is to first, do all you can to avoid negative energy from entering into your being, and into your home and environment. This can be accomplished by eluding and staying away from its sources. Remember, this is done only by your choice, and to pray for those around you who enjoy the company of these destructive forces to find peace and sanctuary in the loving hands of God. And most importantly, to pray to God, our Father, to invoke His dome of white protective light all around you and through you. Also say this prayer for your family and friends: *"Dear Heavenly Father, wrap me in Divine Love and place me in your cradle of light. Put your dome of protection around me and my loved ones this day (night) and watch over us. Bless us, and guide us, and keep us from harm. Amen."* If this prayer to God is said twice daily (morning and night), then the effects of negative energy cannot and will not harm you or your loved ones. Through prayer to God, the Father, you will surely be protected. Without prayer, God will not intervene and impose His will.

Now, as the effects of negative energy cause harm, illness, pain, and disease, the complete opposite is true with the effects of positive energy. All of God's glorious Creation is healed through positive energy. Positive energy works its miraculous forces to bring healing, true happiness, love and peace to all. The frequencies of positive energy are elated and exalted. Positive energy is lofty and divinely powerful. Positive energy is of a high vibration and therefore allows light into a person's soul. Positive energy frequencies are indeed 100% compatible with every embodiment of your being.

Your physical body and all its functions are truly and divinely enhanced by the light speed of vibration or frequency of positive energy. This is because positive energy and all its structure—the light, divine radiant colors and frequencies—are 100% compatible and completely correspond with the body's central nervous system and the immune system. Positive energy harmoniously and divinely balances the electromagnetic system of the human being. Positive energy brings life and power into the DNA strands of the human being. Your DNA strands are etheric, spiritual, and are activated by the light, the radiant colors and the frequencies of positive energy. Through positive energy, these mighty DNA strands will awaken your mind to the universal knowledge that exists in your soul. DNA strands work harmoniously and in conjunction with one another. The more positive energy you invite into your life and into your being, the more powerful its divine effects. The all-powerful and divine positive energy can restore and bring back to life the inactive and dormant DNA strands of the human being. Positive energy empowers every atom and molecule. Positive energy will bring the divine power of health and healing into each and every cell of the physical body. This will repair any damage done by negative energy.

Positive energy creates a state of spiritual bliss for human beings. Beloved souls, affirm yourself daily with positive statements. This creates positive energy. Pray to God and ask Him to bring His positive energy and all its glorious healing and empowering effects into your being and into your everyday life. For when you willfully invite positive energy into your being, your soul will fill with divine love. The more light that is within your soul, the more radiant your being and the brighter your journey to the heavens will be. Positive energy is Divine love, and Divine love is your true life. Glory and praise to our Father, God in Heaven. My love and Violet Flame of purity is offered to all.

Saint Germain,
received by Eve Barbieri

CHAPTER 5

PRAYER

by
The Holy Spirit, Jesus, and Mother Mary

✥ PRAYER ✥

PART I

PRAYER COUNSEL
by The Holy Spirit/The Great White Brotherhood

Greetings, dear one. We, the Brotherhood of God come to counsel you on the subject of prayer.

Much about prayer is misunderstood. True prayer begins in the heart before a word is spoken. It does not consist of repetition or pleading. It is not necessary to plead and persuade God. God knows your heart. He knows your life and He knows your needs. A simple request, made in gratitude for the Father's loving care, is all that is required, and it is yours. To beg and plead hinders prayer in that it is filled with doubt—doubt in the love of the Father, doubt in your worthiness as His child, and doubt that He even pays attention to you. A *fervent* prayer is not a prayer of begging, but of urgent need and much gratitude. Learn from your children. When there is an urgent need, how do they approach you? They are your teachers. Approach God in this same way. If you need comfort, He will be there. If you need help, He will send help. The tone in your voice lets Him know and the cries of your heart reach His ears. When you call 911, do you beg? Or do you state the problem and trust that help is on the way?

Too often, people only pray when they are in trouble and because of guilt. Having not given God much attention in their life, they apologize and then beg forgiveness, and beg some more for what they need. This becomes a familiar pattern that is self-defeating, for the bond of trust never develops. But when you pray, do so with confidence. Believe that you will receive that for which you pray—and more. Expect it. And know it will come at the right time and in the right way. The Father wants you to have joy, and not to be worried and afraid. Be thankful and be happy.

The Great White Brotherhood of God,
received by Romayne de Kanter

INFORMATION ABOUT PRAYER
by Jesus

Greetings and the Lord's blessings to all who dwell on Earth. I am the Lord Jesus, and I am coming through to this oracle today to give to you information and knowledge about prayers, faith, and meditation. As you may know, prayer is talking to God and meditation is going within yourself to listen to God.

First I will begin with information on prayer. Prayer is the method of communicating your thoughts and needs to God, the Father. God already knows all your thoughts and all your needs—this is truth. However, to pray to God allows God to enter into your life and intervene with His divine right order for your highest good. Knowing this may help some of the people on Earth to understand why prayer is so very important. As you know, God, the Father, does not intervene into your lives unless He is asked to do so. So this means that prayer to God, the Father, is your invitation for Him to intervene into your being and into your life with His blessings of love and gifts of spiritual abundance. With prayer to God, you will always be divinely guided and you will never have to conquer life's challenges alone. With prayer, you always have God with you because you have invited Him into your life.

Prayers to God, our Father, change the course of your life for the better. Prayer strengthens your being. Through your faithful prayers to God, the Father, the physical body's immune system and central nervous system functions at a much greater advantage, thereby enhancing the physical body of the human being. Every follicle of hair on the body is nourished with divine love through prayers to God. Every cell that makes up the human body divides and multiplies with great strength and power of love from the Source of all, our God. Every atom and molecule of the human brain is chemically changed and evolves more rapidly through prayer to our Father, God.

With sincere and faithful prayer to God, all of the embodiments of the human being, the physical, emotional, mental and spiritual bodies are greatly enhanced and evolved with a more clear understanding of the love and peace of God. The mind of the third-dimensional human being is taught God's infinite wisdom of the universe when prayers to God and holy meditations are practiced daily. When one communes with God and goes within to receive messages from God and the Holy Spirit, the emotions of this person are stabilized and at peace. The spiritual body is nurtured and nourished through earnest and heartfelt prayers to God, and the willingness to go within the spiritual mind to receive divine guidance and knowledgeable understanding of the universe.

The act of prayer is essential to grow and evolve spiritually. You begin building your foundation of spiritual evolvement and oneness with God by praying to God, our Father. This is vitally important to understand. To live by prayer to God, our Father, you will live for all eternity in God's divine light and love, for prayer opens the doorway to finding God and experiencing God in your life.

GOD HEARS ALL THE PRAYERS OF EVERY HUMAN BEING ON EARTH, REGARDLESS OF THEIR RELIGIOUS BELIEFS. All who wish to sit next to the Lord, our God, may do so. BELOVED ONES, GOD, OUR FATHER, IS ALL RELIGIONS; GOD IS EVERYWHERE. There is not one place in all of God's vast and immeasurable Creation that God refuses to live in. God, the Father, lives and breathes in everything you see and all you may not see. If you wish to call upon me, the Lord Jesus, you may do so at any time, anywhere, for I too live in and am One with God's immense and glorious Creation. I am pleased and privileged to lead you on the golden spiritual path to God, the Father. All prayer is powerful, and there are methods of prayer that generate great power of love energy from God.

The sincerity of prayer to God is most important. You are to show God, the Father deep respect and sincerity when praying to Him. You are to humble yourself to your knees when asking the Father, God, for your prayer requests. This is to be if your situation allows this. Granted, this is not expected from the people of Earth who have any physical body challenges, or if a person is in a particular circumstance or situation and is not able at the time to kneel and pray. During these situations I, Jesus, say to you, pray to God in your mind, for God, the Father, knows what is in your heart. When you plan certain sacred times of your day and kneel to God in prayer, you are communing with God during those sacred moments. This communing with God through prayer is the strongest way for your conscious mind to begin the reconnecting process to God, the Father. Frequent and sincere prayer is how to maintain and keep your connection to God reinforced.

At this time, I, Jesus, wish to bring to your mind some added knowledge concerning a few powerful methods of prayer.

A prayer circle is an immensely powerful form of prayer. There is monumental power generated when family, friends and all who wish to connect with God form a circle of infinite, ever-circulating love energy, and pray together to the Heavenly Father. When all who are in the prayer circle hold hands and pray together to God, this action connects and unites everyone with an infinite circle of light energy. This mighty energy of the prayer circle spirals upward toward the heavens, outward to encompass mass areas of land on the planet, and downward into the core of the Earth. This energy has a balancing effect and can neutralize negative energy, which creates major upheavals in man's societies and in the weather patterns. For a family to pray together in a circle of infinite and rotating love energy, will bring tremendous peace and harmony to the household. When a family prays together to God, the family is united with the power of God's almighty love.

Also, I, Jesus wish to mention another powerful method of prayer. This is the making of an altar. This method involves creating an altar or sacred space in your home. At this altar is where prayers and offerings of gratitude are made for answered prayers. Begin by creating a clean place in your home where sacred and sacramental objects can be displayed. This can include anything cherished by you and that may pertain to your spiritual or religious beliefs. However, it is important to make known, it is well-advised to have a symbol of power at your altar or sacred space. For example, the cross is a symbol which holds within it an immense amount of power. The cross is made up of four of the letter Ls. These four Ls stand for Love, Light, Life, and Law. It is to be understood that the cross will bring to your altar or sacred space (and to your home) the power of Love, the power of Light, the power of Life, and the power of Divine Law. The obelisk and the pyramid are also highly respected symbols of great and mighty power. Your altar or sacred space does not have to be elaborate with items that cost much money. Create within your monetary means, for it is what dwells in your heart that truly matters. You can, if you wish, take some stones from outdoors and arrange them in the symbol of the cross. To write on a piece of paper, "God" and "The Lord Jesus Christ" will bring to your altar and your home great light and love. You can add to your altar or sacred space anything that brings you great joy, or that you find dear to your heart. In addition, any statues or pictures at your altar of my mother Mary, the saints and angels, will bring wondrous power and enlightenment to you, your prayers, and to your home. I encourage you to beautify your altar or sacred space with anything that symbolizes the grace of God's Creation on the planet Earth. For example, plants, flowers, stones, crystals, and perhaps a candle, would make wonderful tributes to your loving and powerful host, planet Earth.

I, the Lord Jesus, will now speak to you about your prayer offerings. A prayer offering is a token of sincere gratitude to God for your prayers being answered. The offering is to be placed upon the altar or sacred space *before* you begin praying to God. **A prayer offering is not to be any money, and a prayer offering is never to be the dead carcass of a sacrificed animal.** The Biblical days of sacrificing animals for the purpose of religious rituals are long over and not to be practiced in this day and age—*ever*. This is law, with **no exceptions.** To sacrifice an animal in the name of the Lord, our God would be a terrible sin against God and all of God's Creation, including yourself. A prayer offering to God is to be benign and good-natured, and given with love and purity of the heart. I will give some examples of acceptable prayer offerings: some herbs and spices, such as parsley, thyme, or a bay leaf from this magnificent and grand planet Earth; a piece of bread, or a handful of birdseed to give to the noble birds who sing their celestial songs for all to hear and enjoy. Or to write on a piece of paper, "A kind word to all I speak to this day." Then you offer one of these things, or something else you may be inspired to give at the altar *before* praying. (Remember, whatever you give must be good-natured or holy, and of the Light). After your prayer to God is finished, you can use the spices to flavor the cooking of food for your family, or spread the bread or seed on the ground for the birds of glory to eat. If your offering is a promise of kindness, such as a kind word or helping hand to your fellow man, then this must be carried out. This is an extremely powerful form of sincere prayer.

Prayer is not to be looked upon as a chore, but as the way to connect to your true reality, which is your spiritual path to God, the Father. Prayer to God, the Father, brings light into your spirit and into your soul. The examples of the prayer methods that I have given to you are ways to better yourself and your life. These formalities of prayer will give you enlightenment and bring to you new insights. The practice of these prayer methods will establish for you a daily routine of connecting to God, the Father, through prayer. Sincere daily prayers to God will greatly enrich your life.

Beloved ones, pray to God for yourself. Pray to God for your family. Pray to God for your friends. Pray to God for the animals of the world. Pray to God for peace in the world. And yes, beloved ones, pray to God for your enemies. For what you pray for others, for your family, for your friends, and also your enemies, will surely come to you first. When you pray to God to send His Divine Love and Divine Light to your enemies, you will not only help your enemies, you will help yourself. The anger you feel inside of you will be released into the ethers through your sincere prayers of love, mercy, and forgiveness for your enemies. You will find total peace through prayers to God.

At this time, it is important to make clear that by simply talking to God, the Father, in your mind, you are also praying to Him. God, the Father, knows all of your thoughts and He hears every word of every language spoken. And God answers every thought given to Him and every word spoken to Him. Even though you may not think this is true—this is absolute truth. All things given to God are done by God through Divine Right Order. What this means specifically is that all prayers to God, the Father are answered at the perfect time for your highest good. God, our Father, Creator of all the Heavens and Universes, is total 100% pure perfection. Any problem, burden, dilemma, or unsettling circumstance given to God will be done in the highest perfection. All *you* need to do, to allow this to become a reality for you, is to have 100% faith in God. All prayers said to me, the Lord Jesus Christ, are given to Our Heavenly Father, for God is the first and only true Source of all Creation.

My love and light shines upon the glorious planet Earth and all who dwell there.

The Lord Jesus Christ,
received by Eve Barbieri

PART 3:

PEACE THROUGH PRAYER
by Mother Mary

Hello, beloved of the Father. This is Mother Mary, and I have come to speak to you at this time concerning inner peace. When there is peace in your life, and peace in your home, it will be as an oasis in the desert. The world has very little peace, and turmoil is everywhere. Without peace, there is strife and there is illness of all kinds, physical as well as emotional and mental. People seek peace through the use of drugs and medications. This however, does not bring *true* peace. True peace comes only from God, our Father, and is given through prayer.

Prayer cleanses the heart and mind of daily concerns and worries, as well as the seemingly constant irritations that are a part of life. These all leave their mark, so to speak, on a person's sense of well-being. These "little" problems, if not brought to God in daily prayer to be cleansed and purified, are then allowed to build upon each other. The mind becomes increasingly burdened until it is in a state of overwhelm. Anger, usually directed at vulnerable loved ones, is a frequent result, as is depression.

I cannot stress enough the importance of bringing your concerns to God daily in prayer. Understand beloved souls, prayer does not always bring relief from your problems. There are lessons to be learned. However, prayer brings a sense of peace *within* your problems, and also a new perspective in which to view these problems. You cannot control another being, but you are able to adjust your attitude and perspective. Oftentimes, this alone will eliminate the problem, for it was the attitude that caused it in the first place.

If you live in anger or depression, which is anger turned inward, start your daily prayer by asking God to show you what is really bothering you—and why. A journal or diary that you write in daily about the events, feelings, and related issues that came up during the day will be most helpful in giving some insight into what to bring into your prayers. This can also be in the form of a letter to God, telling Him, as you would a friend, about your day and your concerns. There are many ways and methods of prayer, and all are honored by God, our Father.

Wherever I have appeared, my message has always been to pray and especially to pray for peace. Peace will come as your prayers to God increase. It comes into your hear and mind first. Then as you pray also for peace in the world and among nations, the collective consciousness is affected. When there is war *within* man, there will be war *among* men. When there is war among men, it results in great suffering and loss of spiritual advancement. War brings with it hate and strife that lasts for decades, even centuries. It serves no one, heals no one, and is only self-destructive. The path to God, however noble in the confused minds of men, is not paved with the dead bodies of those of a different faith, belief, or nationality. This is not God's will. All are God's children, and all are precious to Him. The true purpose of prayer is to be able to see through the eyes of God, to come into the oneness of all life. In this sacred oneness, there is only love.

To many of you, this bringing of your concerns to God in daily prayer is a new concept. Some of you recite certain prayers every day. This is good, but more is needed. Talk to God about your concerns, and talk from your heart. This is true prayer. As each day is different, so each day your prayers will be different. If you need help and guidance in this new way to pray, I am always available to help, as are the angels of God, and you can call on us at any time.

May the peace of God fill your being and your life.

Mother Mary, mother of Jesus,
received by Romayne de Kanter

PART 4:

DAILY PRAYERS

PRAYER FOR PROTECTION
by Archangel Michael

Dear Heavenly Father, wrap me in Divine Love and place me in your cradle of light. Put your dome of protection around me and my loved ones this day (night) and watch over us. Bless us, and guide us, and keep us from harm. Amen.

PRAYER FOR GUIDANCE
by The Lord Jesus Christ

Heavenly Father, God, I pray for you to guide me this day, and to embrace me with your Divine Wisdom. I ask, Father, God, for your White Light and your Divine Knowledge to be one with me. And I pray, dear Lord, for my God-mind to become one with my conscious mind, so that I am forever enlightened. Thank you Father, God. Amen.

PRAYER FOR SERENITY
by The Lord Jesus Christ

Father, God in Heaven, I pray to you this day for your peace and serenity to enter into my heart and mind. I pray for your peace to encompass all my being and all that I do. I ask dear God, that your White Light of serenity become one with my soul, so that I may feel the peacefulness of your heavens. I thank you Lord God, for hearing my prayer. Amen.

(more prayers on next two pages)

FOOD BLESSING
by Saint Germain

Dear Heavenly Father, I (we) thank you for our food. I (we) ask you God, to bless this food with your White Light and your Love, and we pray for your blessings to all of your wonderful Creation. Amen.

PRAYER FOR THE ANIMALS
by Saint Francis of Assisi

Dear Heavenly Father, Creator of our world, I pray for the safety and well-being of all animals on Earth. I ask you, God, to hold every suffering animal on Earth in your arms and heal them with your White Light and your Love. I pray for the collective consciousness of mankind to be raised so that all people are able to see the pain and suffering animals must endure at the hand of man. May mankind and animals unite once again, and live in harmony for all eternity on planet Earth. I pray Father, God, for all people to find your love in their hearts, and respect all living things. I thank you, God, for hearing my prayer and for your answer. Amen.

PRAYER FOR WORLD PEACE
by Mother Mary, mother of Jesus

Dear God, our Father in Heaven, please place the thought of everlasting peace into every heart and mind of mankind. I pray, Father, for your miracles of peace to spread throughout all the land on Earth, so that we may know of wars as only a memory to be released into your healing light of love. May all who live on planet Earth feel at this time, the Golden Age of Peace that is forthcoming. Father, God, may all who breathe in this world be encompassed by your love. I thank you Father, God, for hearing my prayer and for your answer. Amen.

JESUS' PRAYER
by The Lord Jesus Christ

Loving Savior, Son of God, who in the glory of the cross now rules at the right hand of the Father, intercede for us and cleanse us from all unrighteousness. Place your teachings in the core of our hearts, and show us how to live in your perfect love and peace. Let your light shine in us and bless the world. Amen.

Chapter 6

PROTECTION

by
Archangel Michael

✤ PROTECTION ✤

Greetings, beloved children of God. This is Archangel Michael. Today I wish to speak to you concerning protection.

As you go about your daily sojourn, there are unseen influences that affect you. These are energy forms of various kinds. Some are positive. Some are negative. Some are just different— neither positive or negative—but they are incompatible with you and make you uncomfortable, somewhat like wearing a garment that does not fit just right. It is what you might term as irritating.

As you go about your activities of the day, you encounter many people. Some only brush by you. Others interact on a more significant level with you. But all encounters leave their mark, so to speak, on your personal energy field.

Beloved souls, all that exists is composed of energy. There are symbols in your world, as in the world of business, that you see in the media and on your drive to work. These, too, have energies attached to them. For example, when you see a soft drink ad, you suddenly become thirsty. This is because these energies carry within them "thought drops." Some people who are, shall we say, somewhat "awake" will be aware of this. However, most of you are spiritual sleepwalkers, in that you go through the motions of your day preoccupied with your own thoughts (which by the way, are also affecting others), and totally unaware of the energy exchanges that are taking place around you.

Many people are concerned with "germs" and coming into contact with people who are sick. They worry that they may "catch" something. Yet, they are totally oblivious to the thought drops and energies they are "catching," which can be far more detrimental than a brief illness.

Have you ever felt sad and didn't know why? Nothing happened to cause you to feel this way, but still you are "down in the dumps," as you say. Perhaps you feel a bit out of sorts, like you "got out of bed on the wrong side" as the saying goes. You snap at people for no good reason and people avoid you. You don't like being this way, yet you don't know how you got like this, or how to fix it. You say, "I need a vacation," or some such excuse. Well, in a way this is true. You need to stop and get to a quiet place where you can hear your true self again.

BELOVED SOULS, THE QUALITY OF YOUR LIFE IS A RESULT OF THE ENERGIES YOU ALLOW INTO IT. Understand that when you allow violence into your life, whether you associate with those of a violent nature, or through the television set in your home, the effect is the same. Violence is violence—no matter what the source—and the thought drops of violence are still affecting you.

The point is, you can catch thought drops from those around you. You can pick up how they are feeling, consciously or unconsciously. Your commercials and ads in your entertainment are other ways that thought drops influence you. Many of you desire to lose weight, but have been unsuccessful. I would suggest that all the fast food ads might be the overpowering factor in your failure at this endeavor. The established system is geared toward greed, and not toward your best interests. They invent a disease, convince you that you have it, and then sell you a very expensive pill to cure it—and most of you buy into it readily. Such is the power of advertising and the manipulating of your mind and energies. If you are told often enough that you are sick, sooner or later you will begin to believe it. If peace, love and faith were marketed in this way, what a different and blessed world this would be!

You, dear souls, have unwittingly given your power away to the television, the advertisers, and the people around you. It is time to awaken and take your power back. You can protect your home, your body, and your mind. I will give you some suggestions.

The first thing you must do is become aware of how you are being affected. Ask God for this gift of awareness. If you don't know a problem exists, you will not look for the solution.

Now, in some cultures there is a ceremony called "smudging." In this ceremony prayers are said and sacred herbs are lit and then allowed to smolder, creating a fair amount of smoke. This smoke is carried throughout the house and applied around each person. This process cleans the area and the people's energy field. You will feel lighter and more "free" when this is done. This is usually done with sage, for it has powerful cleansing properties.

Then you must pray and ask God for His white light of protection. This is your Divine Shield against harm. You must renew this request every morning and night. It is a daily thing. Ask your angel to remind you. If you forget, and find yourself feeling out of balance in some way, ask God to remove this misplaced energy and take it into the light. Then renew your protection.

If you ever get an inner warning of danger, if you are ever concerned for a loved one who is late in arriving—indeed, any time you are worried about yourself or another, immediately invoke God's dome of protection. It is yours for the asking. To go without your protective shield is like going without your clothes, only more so. Think of it in this way.

This is a good habit to form and teach to your children. They are even more susceptible to energy forms than you are, for their energy centers are more vulnerable.

Now, here is a tip for those of you who are attempting to shed those unwanted pounds. I would suggest that you collect the ads and logos of all the fast food restaurants you can find from magazines and so forth. Cut the logos out and with a bold marking pen, write the words "I am slim, trim, and healthy," right on top of the logo itself. Place them on your bathroom mirror, your doors, your refrigerator—anywhere you can readily see them. After awhile, your mind will be reprogrammed and give you the new message whenever you see that logo.

You see, beloved souls, this is how to take back your power. Awareness is the first step. Then set aside some quiet moments so you can receive guidance from your God-self on how to become the Self-master you were meant to be. Guard your mind and do not give your power away, or take anyone else's power away. The power of suggestion, the power of choice... they are your tools to build a good life. Guard them well and pray always for protection.

I am only a call away and always at your service. May the light of God fill your mind with truth.

PRAYER

Dear Heavenly Father, wrap me in Divine Love and place me in your cradle of light. Put your dome of protection around me and my loved ones this day (night) and watch over us. Bless us and guide us and keep us from harm. Amen.

Archangel Michael,
received by Romayne de Kanter

CHAPTER 7

COMPASSION

by
Mother Mary

✛ COMPASSION ✛

Greetings, beloved children. This is Mother Mary, and today I want to speak to you about compassion. True compassion is a gift from the Father, the giver of all good. The Father has compassion for all of His Creation. It is an aspect of Divine Love that brings healing and comfort to the afflicted.

When you show compassion to another being or animal, or any living thing, you are in the beauty of the Father's love. All beings feel this loving energy as it extends from you—even those who are not receiving your direct care. This tenderest of love vibrations blesses all that are anywhere near it. I, as your loving Mother, manifest this attribute of God, the Father, and have been privileged to be the vehicle of compassion through which God extends His mercy.

There is much pain on Earth. Most of it is self-inflicted. This is not pleasing to God. He does not wish His children to suffer any more than you want this for your own children. But there is cause and effect. The right choice brings blessings. Wrong choices—choices that go against the laws of God and nature— bring curses and suffering. Again, dear children of the Father, it is your choices that affect your life and the lives of those around you. The Father takes no pleasure in suffering and cruelty. It is a most difficult way for you to learn, for when you are within the pain, you don't often know how you ended up there. The process and choices leading up to your present circumstances must be examined closely in order to receive the gift of truth and enlightenment.

God does not cause you to suffer. God does not punish you or get back at you. You do that to yourself. God loves you at all times, even when you make a mistake or a foolish choice. He is full of compassion towards you.

Dear ones, if you see an animal hit by an automobile, do you not have compassion for this animal? It may have made a mistake by running into the road, but that doesn't matter. All that matters is that this animal is in pain and needs help. And so the Father's heart goes out to His little ones in pain, full of compassion and desire to help. You need have no fear or hesitate to reach out to Him for comfort. The love of humans may wax cold, but God's love is constant and never fails. To lean on God and trust in His love and mercy will bring you through all your trials and heartaches, back into joy and peace. Have compassion for yourself. Forgive yourself and be gentle with your soul. God will dry all your tears and heal all your wounds. It is His good pleasure to do so.

I, Mary, mother of Jesus, urge you to pray for all the souls that suffer upon this planet. Pray for an increase in compassion and healing love to be released into the hearts of all mankind. Many children, elderly, and helpless people and animals are forced to live in abusive and deplorable conditions due to a lack of compassion by their caregivers. As my son said, "What you have done to the least of these, you did it to me," for God lives in each soul and feels their pain. Pray much for the gift of compassion, for greed and selfishness rule and take their toll upon the helpless. This is not pleasing to God, and an accounting will be taken. There will be much weeping by the perpetrators. God sees all things in truth. NO THING is hidden from Him. Live each moment in the light of that knowledge so you may stand blameless before Him. When you forget this and think God does not see, then you deceive yourself. I point this out, not to put fear into you, but only to steer you onto the right path—the path to God.

Be kind to one another and follow the Golden Rule. Pray for the gift of compassion in all that you care for. Everyone cares for someone or something, even if it is only your home. If you have compassion for your home, you will not kick in the walls when you get angry.

I stand ready to assist you in these matters if you will but ask for me. Open your hearts to receive more of God's love and you will be blessed and healed. I hold you always in my heart.

Mother Mary, mother of Jesus,
received by Romayne de Kanter

CHAPTER 8

FORGIVENESS

by
Mother Mary

✛ FORGIVENESS ✛

Greetings and my love to all the world and God's Creation. This is Mother Mary, mother of Jesus. Today I wish to speak to you about forgiveness. Forgiveness is essential in your life if you wish to be close to God, the Father, and have a strong connection with Him. In today's world, you the people have been programmed into believing forgiveness is difficult. This is not truth. If one has the love and peace of God, the Father, in his/her heart, then dear ones, forgiveness comes to you as second nature. There must dwell in your mind and heart true love, compassion, and understanding for there to be true forgiveness. Understand, dear ones, no one on your planet Earth at this time is without sin. Only my son, Jesus, is the Christed Being, the One without sin. Every one of you have made mistakes during this lifetime and many lifetimes ago. These mistakes teach you and others in many ways. One of those ways is the way of forgiveness. To forgive is to let go of anger, blame, and hatred for something that you or someone else has done in the past. A clear definition of forgiving is to *let go of fear.*

When you forgive, you release all of those negative emotions which are inside of your being. These emotions are very harmful to your mental, physical, emotional, and spiritual bodies. To harbor these feelings keeps all of you, all of your embodiments out of balance, not in harmony. This is one great cause of disease today in the people of the world. Most people do not wish to release these harmful emotions toward others and themselves. Please understand, beloved ones, once you start the process of forgiveness, of letting go of the blame and hatred, then the body can start the wonderful process of healing itself.

This process is begun by praying to the Father, God in Heaven. Understand and please know in your hearts, *GOD LOVES YOU WITH THE MOST POWERFUL AND ENDLESS LOVE THERE IS.* God is always there for you. He hears every prayer, every cry for help. God knows the pain you have endured at the hand of another. God sees, hears, and knows all. Find God now through prayer. Ask Him for the guidance to forgive those who have hurt you. Always know in your hearts, dear ones, children of God, all things are possible through God. God can and does fix everything if you ask Him to. Forgiveness brings to your life a whole new understanding, a new perspective of why things happened to you—why the wrongdoing was allowed. God can bring this knowledge to you individually through prayer. However, I will give some basic knowledge at this time.

As you know, in this world and all worlds there is free will and free choice. God does not force His will upon you. Because of this, people can do and have done much harm to other people and animals and themselves. Bring into your understanding that if you were the victim of wrongdoing, then that act has taught you something very valuable. At the very least it has taught you that a strong connection with God is where healing of the physical, emotional, and mental body begins. It has taught you that you are not vulnerable if you pray to the Heavenly Father for protection. Pray for yourselves and your children that Our God will protect them and you from harm. Ask God to put my son's Christ Light around yourself and your children at all times. Pray for this every day. When you forgive, your heart opens up with love and goodness that heals not only yourself, but brings healing to those involved, which can prevent more harm from happening again.

I know this may seem difficult at first. There is much resentment to get through in your emotional body. Your emotional and mental bodies say, "Why did this happen to me?" Because, my dear ones, you allowed it to happen to you. There are many reasons why you allowed this to happen to you. This may be part of your karma clearing itself, or maybe you chose to come here to be the wonderful gift of learning for someone else. Allow me, Mother Mary, to explain more. When you are in spirit, before you incarnate into this life on Earth, you choose much of what you are going to experience. You choose what gender you will be, what race you will be, what part of the world you will be birthed into. You choose your parents and yes, beloved souls, you choose some of the abuse you will endure in this lifetime. This may be for the purpose of balancing karma, or you chose to be the one someone else may abuse so this other person may realize how abuse affects people. By being the gift of knowledge for another person who abuses to learn from, *you are and will be blessed by God, the Father.*

Understanding this may help you to know that if you pray to God for love and healing, you will receive very powerful healing and guidance to start the forgiving process. All of you people on the planet Earth can receive messages from our Loving Father. All you need to do is ask. God does not speak to one child and not to the other. He speaks to all of His children. All you must do is pray and listen. The guidance will come into your life. The best way to start to hear clearly is through meditation—to sit and be still. To allow your mind to flood itself with thoughts and emotions. This is normal to have happen at first. However, as you keep meditating, your mind will become clear, clear enough to hear or get impressions of thoughts and guidance. If you wish, you can hold a crystal in your left hand. This will bring to your mind much awareness. In your prayers and meditations, ask for God—and only God—to give you His love and guidance. This insures you will hear and/or receive messages from the highest Source, our God. God's messages serve only your highest good. By doing this every day, you will receive healing and support beyond what you could ever imagine. Your heart will be filled with total peace.

May I say, this process does not happen overnight. Take for example, when a person has their skin and flesh cut, there is a period of time before the wound is completely healed. Healing is done in stages. There may be some days when you may feel emotionally or physically worse than other days. This is part of the healing process. Do not despair, beloved ones, if you have a period of time when you find it difficult to forgive. Pray to God. Tell Him how you feel. You will have more love and more healing given to you immediately at that time. Always remember, God loves you with the most powerful love that exists. God, the Ascended Masters and the archangels and angels of God are always here for you. All you need to do is ask. By forgiving and praying for those who have wronged you, you release from your physical body and your soul all the pain that keeps you feeling down.

Forgiveness is uplifting. By asking God for help and guidance to completely forgive both yourself and others, you bring to yourself a "new lease on life" so to speak. The expression, "This is the first day of the rest of my life," rings true. When you forgive and find in your heart total peace and love, then you have conquered all of the negative emotions that cause illness and disease in the mind, heart, and physical body. You have strengthened your connection to God, the Father. To forgive, to completely forgive and have peace in your heart, brings you closer into your God-mind. Your God-mind is always a part of your human mind. However, for your God-mind to be activated into your physical mind, you must have a strong connection with God, the Father. Your God-mind is one of love and peace and the giving of yourself *to* yourself and others. Forgiveness plays an invaluable role in the re-connecting to the God-mind.

You and your God-mind were one, together and pure, when you were created by God. Our Father God only creates pure love. However, your God-mind connection has been somewhat weakened by many, many years of density. Your God-mind is that part of your mind that dwells in the Heavens with the Lord God. You see, beloved children of God, you are *always* one with God. Your own mind, your human mind and the thought of being separated from God is the only obstacle that keeps you from being one with God and your God-mind. This connection with your physical mind and your God-mind can be strengthened only through daily prayer and meditation.

To ask God for forgiveness for your sins is a great place to start. All of you people of the planet Earth have sinned. Once you have repented to God (told Him you are sorry for all of your sins and to ask Him for forgiveness), then you can ask God, the Father, to help you forgive those who have done you wrong in some way. No person on Earth is perfect. Only God is pure perfection. The anger and hatred you feel can be taken away only by God's pure light and love. Have no fear. Fear is the opposite of faith. Put all of your trust in God to help you forgive yourself and to forgive others. The love and support from the Heavens is within your reach. My love is given to all the world.

Mother Mary, mother of Jesus,
received by Eve Barbieri

✛ CHAPTER 9 ✛

FAITH

by
The Lord Jesus Christ

✛ FAITH ✛

PART I:

TRUE FAITH

Greetings and blessings to all of God's children. This is Jesus, and I have a message to give to all concerning *true faith*.

There are many confusing beliefs concerning what faith is and how it works. Oftentimes what people term faith is not faith at all, but an effort on the part of humans to persuade God to see things or some matter the way they do. God's perspective, dear ones, is not limited. He does not have "tunnel vision" the way human beings do. You cannot have true faith that God will perform the way you want Him to. That is not faith at all. However, it often masquerades as such. This is where confusion comes in, and often results in the loss of whatever true faith a person had. Let me give you an example.

Suppose you are sick and are praying to God for healing. Now, if in your mind, you think that God will just miraculously cure you, this is not true faith. It is misguided faith, for your understanding of God and His ways is lacking. God may choose to answer your prayer by directing you to a very gifted physician, but with your misunderstanding, you cannot see the hand of God guiding you. So when the answer does not come from the direction you expect, you despair and think that God has not heard your prayer, or will not answer it. You may even think you have committed some great sin and that God has turned away from you. This error in thinking has caused great pain and suffering and even death in some cases. You cannot try to force God to do something your way and call it faith.

99

So what then is *true faith*? True faith is the knowing deep within your heart and soul that God loves you and hears every prayer. God's love is with each and every one of His children at every moment. The sinner who cries out to God is answered instantly, as well as the saint. This is truth, and you can have faith, true faith, in this divine truth. You can have faith that even before your prayer is finished, the answer is on its way to you. This is also true faith.

But, dear ones, you cannot have *true* faith in when or how the answer will come. You must be alert, expecting the answer to come to you from any direction and through any means. Let me give you another example.

Perhaps you need some money to purchase an item you need and you take the matter to God in prayer. God can answer in many ways. Someone may just give you the item you need, or God may send you the money by means of a gift from someone you know, or God could send you an employment opportunity where you can earn this money, or perhaps God will send someone who will want to buy some item you have, or trade with you for the item you want. So you see, dear ones, when you bring a concern to God in prayer, you cannot have true faith that the answer will come in only one way. You must allow God to work His perfect will in answering your prayer. Knowing and expecting that the answer is on its way is *true* faith, for your faith rests in the goodness of God and His almighty love for you. When you pray, always ask to be able to recognize the answer when it arrives, so that you do not miss the opportunities that Spirit brings.

True faith is simple and extremely powerful. Doubt in God's unconditional and almighty love for you is the greatest deterrent to faith and receiving the answers to your prayers. You, as God's child, are always and ever very special and very loved. Allow this truth to rest within your being and become a part of you. When you can live your life with this knowledge and perspective, true faith will also be a part of your daily life.

Understand and know, dear ones, that God, the Father, loves to hear from His children. God rejoices in each and every one of you and is most happy when invited into your life. Again I say to you, God does not condemn you ever. God only loves, God forgives, and God blesses. God is the most loving Father you could ever imagine. There is no need for you to "go it alone," for all you need is just a prayer away. Pray with confidence, for there is no prayer that goes unanswered.

My peace is upon each of you.

The Lord Jesus Christ,
received by Romayne de Kanter

KNOWLEDGE ABOUT FAITH

I am the Lord Jesus Christ, and I wish to give you knowledge of Faith. Faith is not tangible. It is not an object to hold in your hand. Your faith is a part of you. It is a major part of who you are. It is an energy and an emotion inside of you that connects your soul to God, the Father. Faith is your knowing inside of you that God is always with you and His love for you is unconditional and eternal. Faith in God, the Father, is your knowledge of God and your confidence in God. Faith is a powerful and mighty force of connective energy from the physical body to God, the Father. Faith is an element of love.

The importance of faith is astronomical. The importance of faith is that it extends out into space and encompasses the ethers of space with its powerful, positive energy. Beloved ones, know this: Your prayers to God, the Father, are answered through your faith. It is through positive thought-form energy that God works His miracles. It is your faith in God that brings your prayers into a reality for you.

Faith is your stronghold, your defense against all evil. This is because faith—true 100% faith in God, the Father—makes your connection to God strong and durable. Faith brings light into your being. *Faith is the opposite of fear.* Your faith in God is your trust in God. Faith is your assurance that God, the Father will answer your prayers. When you pray to God, the Father, and you have complete trust and faith in Him, then beloved souls, God will surely answer your prayer.

Beloved ones, always trust in God. Have complete faith in God. Your faith in God will bring God to you. God is always with you. This is truth. But you see, beloved souls, it is your *faith*—that is, *your belief* and *your knowing* that God is always with you—and it is this complete faith in God that brings you into the oneness with God our Creator. Go in peace, be in faith. All things are forever possible with God, our Creator. Praise our Lord God in Heaven.

The Lord Jesus Christ,
received by Eve Barbieri

CHAPTER 10

MEDITATION

by
The Lord Jesus Christ

✣ MEDITATION ✣

I, The Lord Jesus Christ, wish to bring to your mind some enlightenment on the subject of meditation. To meditate is to release the mind into the Alpha state of consciousness. The Alpha state is a natural state, an inborn part of the human mind. The Alpha state is the inner-conscious mind. Meditation is astral traveling into other dimensions. To meditate is to become completely still, and go within your inner self, your inner mind, to listen to the messages from God, the Father. This is how I listened to God when I walked the Earth two thousand years ago. Through meditation, I received almighty messages, information, and knowledge from God, the Father. Meditation is a vital part of your connection to God. Your inner peace, this all powerful energy that exists within you, is surfaced into your physical body when you become still and go within to hear the words of God.

Meditation is very simple. This amazing and grand communicating energy with God does not require any special skills or schooling. Any human being can meditate, if they so desire. All that is truly necessary is to deep breathe five or six times until you feel at peace, and drink water—*only water*—(about eight ounces). To consume water in its pure form will help balance the electromagnetic system of the human body. Consumption of water by humans also neutralizes negative thought-forms that have been programmed into the mind, which affect the brain and the physical body. Deep breathing expands your aura, which is essential to meditate in a true, inner-conscious state. After breathing deeply and drinking water, become comfortable, calm, and quiet, and allow yourself to relax. Now, at this time it is very important to keep breathing and to remember to breathe throughout your meditating experience. Depending on your individual lifestyle, your mind may become inundated with various thoughts. *Do not be alarmed.* Instead, allow this natural process of your mental and emotional body to work its course. This is the mind cleansing itself. The emotional and mental bodies will, at times, need to be cleared. The subconscious mind, along with the conscious mind, will hold on to many thoughts and experiences that have not been resolved. At this time, ask God and me, Jesus, for assistance. Ask for love and protection from God, the Father, and me, the Lord Jesus. These requests will be granted to you instantly, and this will greatly enhance your meditating experience. Once the mind has cleared away the now more resolved thoughts and experiences, you are free to enter into the Kingdom of God.

When the mind is settled and at peace, your inner door is opened. Meditating is entering the Kingdom of God's universe within you. Some very advanced meditators can astral travel and visit other realms and dimensions, visit with departed loved ones, and control bodily functions. But for now, we will start at the beginning. If you wish, you can picture yourself in a beautiful garden, or visualize yourself on the top of the highest mountain. And it is important to bring your five senses into your meditating experience. Touch a flower, smell the flowers in your garden, or feel the snow on top of the snow-capped mountain. Deep breathe and smell the clean air. You may think this is only your imagination, and that this is not real. Beloved souls, do not be fooled! Your imagination is what unlocks your inner door to the universe. It is your imagination that is your subconscious mind. And it is through the subconscious mind that your God-mind is activated. It is through your God-mind that you are able to hear God and enter into the Kingdom of Heaven. The subconscious mind is the part of your mind that does not belong to, or is limited to, the third-dimensional reality. Your subconscious mind knows no linear time and does not abide by the laws of physics. That is why there is so much subliminal programming of the subconscious minds of the mass population in your world today. There are people who have discovered and mastered techniques on how to wrongfully manipulate the subconscious minds of people. This wrongful and evil subliminal programming is ruled by the Dark Side to make people think and believe what the Dark Side wants them to believe for the purpose of control. The Dark Forces, along with the people of Earth who side with darkness, wish to control and have dominion over the inner minds of people to execute their (the Dark Side's) destructive will. This is another one of the many reasons why it is vital to pray to God and keep your connection to God open and strong through prayer, faith, and meditation. For by living your life with a strong connection to God, you will *not* fall victim to these unscrupulous acts done by those who wish to control the minds of others.

When you are completely relaxed and have visualized yourself in a wonderful place, ask God to give you His Divine Wisdom and to lead you with His almighty guidance. Ask God, the Father, to keep you in His White Light of Protection and then wait to hear messages from our Father, all the while breathing. It is vitally important to keep your breath strong during meditation. The more often you meditate, the easier and more profound each experience will be. For some people, the more profound and wondrous experiences will take some time. Be patient and pray, beloved souls, for all will be done in its due time.

Meditation will enhance your life greatly. A new sense of peace and a feeling of tranquility will become a part of your being. With daily meditation, you will know and always be confident that the Lord God is with you and He is communicating with you. Through meditation you will receive great enlightenment and true guidance from God. Divine meditation is a life-changing and life-saving experience for you to behold. My love and my light encompasses all the world.

The Lord Jesus Christ,
received by Eve Barbieri

✣ CHAPTER II ✣

KARMA

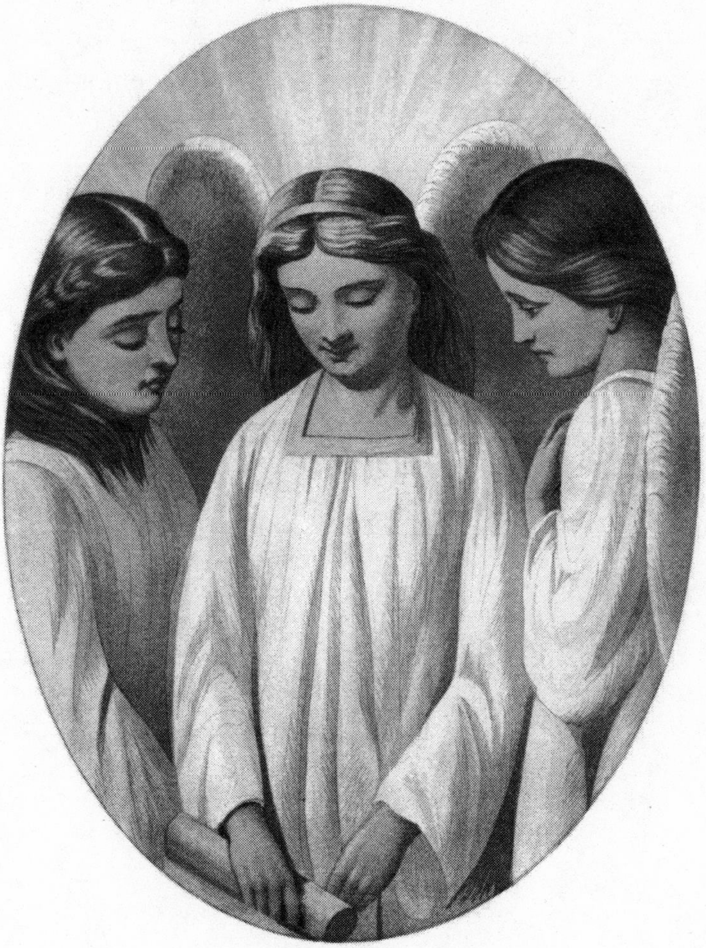

by
Saint Germain

✤ KARMA ✤

Many greetings and wonderful wishes of love. This is Saint Germain. The topic of this chapter is *karma*, what it is and how it affects your life and the lives of those involved. In your world, the planet Earth, human beings have the expression ,"What goes around comes around." THIS IS ABSOLUTE TRUTH. That is why there is a better rule: "Do unto others as you would have them do unto you." Karma is payment, so to speak, for what you do or have done. There is good karma and bad karma. There is instant karma and long-term karma. As you would guess, instant karma takes place almost immediately. An example of this would be if you were to have a negative thought about someone and just after that time of the thought, someone—whether it be that person or someone else—will send a negative thought to you. For example, if someone cuts in front of your car in traffic, and you yell obscenities at them, not realizing this was not intentionally done out of disrespect, then the next time you do the same—cut off another car, not seeing them—they will return the karma. *One of the great laws of the Universe is, "What you give out will come back to you."* Jesus, our Lord, says in the Bible, "Do not be concerned with what goes in; be concerned with what comes out." What comes out of you is truly *you*.

If a person has judgments of others and prejudice about others, and anger toward other people, then that person will have these emotions given back to them stronger than when they were given out. There are a few references in this book about the boomerang. This is the easiest analogy we can give you so you may understand the truth about karma. Understand, dear ones, children of God, when one throws out a boomerang, this device builds up speed. It increases in intensity, therefore sending it back to the person who threw it with a faster and more powerful impact. Karma works precisely in the same manner. When someone sends out anger, that anger builds, and will come back to them stronger and more harmful. The same is true for love. When a person sends out love to another—true love, in its pure form (not love that is mistaken for lust; that is not the same)... I am speaking about love, God-love in the form of kindness, compassion and heartfelt giving, then that person will receive back to them wonderful, fabulous blessings of love from God. God is the First Source of all love. True love is the power to create all living things. What this means to you is that what you put out to others and the planet will dictate how and what your life will be. The events that take place in your life depend on your karma.

Long-term karma is when a deed was done to another—a person, an animal, or any living thing—that was of great harm and the scales of justice must be balanced. Yes, dear ones, there are scales of justice here in the heavens. It is here in the heavens that true justice is served—without fail. Long-term karma may be balanced in one lifetime, or it may take many lifetimes for the scales to be evenly balanced. What I, Saint Germain, am saying to you is that the choices you make in your life here on planet Earth will bring to you either great pain or great love.

Truly knowing this is very important. This is why, when you hear on your television news of a person being murdered and you wonder how God could ever allow such a terrible thing to happen to an innocent person, think to yourself first, before blaming God, the Father, that in a past life they may not have been so innocent. Their murder in this lifetime is restitution for what they may have done in a past lifetime. *Judge not God,* for you do not know each person's life plan. Karma is in harmony with Divine Order. Divine Order consists of remitting and letting go of the past sins so that forgiveness, forgiving yourself, can take place. The laws of your land on Earth are different than God's universal laws in the heavens.

To understand this better, I will say that every life, every animal and person, comes into this world with a plan—everyone, even the "bums" who live on the street. Their plan may have been to know what it is to experience life as a person of little or no monetary wealth. In past lives, this person could have been very wealthy and put all his trust, energy, and focus on his/her large sums of money. When one does this (puts all their focus on money and what it can bring to them), many times they are unkind to those people who have less than they. This person may have seen and understood their behavior in their life review when he/she died and crossed over into spirit. Now this person has come into this Earth life with a plan, to know what it is to experience their life as a bum. This is part of their long-term karma, the long-term understanding. Not every person who portrays a bum in this lifetime is fulfilling their karma, but yes, for some this is indeed the reason.

The same goes for violent crimes. Some—not all, but unfortunately many—of the murders that happen on this planet happen because karma is involved. Understand, beloved souls, much fear exists in the minds and hearts of men on this planet Earth. Fear generates anger; anger leads to violent crimes. In order for someone to commit any violent crime, especially murder, they must—by their own doing, by their own mindset—disconnect themselves from God, the Father. The people who seem to be innocent and are the victims of violent crimes, such as murder, may have done horrible acts of violence in a past life and come into this life with the plan that they will be the victim. They will know and feel and understand the terror and pain this act caused someone else (their victim) to feel. This is the reason why God does not stop this act of darkness—this terrible act done unto those who appear not to deserve it.

God has given every human being—all beings—free will and free choice. Our God, the Father, Creator of all the Heavens and Worlds, does not control your choices and actions. This is why we advise you to keep your connection with God strong. Pray to God. Ask God for protection and guidance, for help in making the choices that are best for you and for your highest good. By doing this every day—keeping your heart open to God's love and guidance—you can bring to your life God's blessings and eliminate fear so that your life is enhanced by the love and blessings of God. Without fear in your mind and in your life, bad karma will not and cannot exist for you in your life. Your lifetime and lifetimes to come can be forever changed for the absolute highest good if you take that step to be one with God, the Father. Change your mindset from one of fear and all the negative emotions that fear brings into your heart and mind—hatred, prejudice, anger, and ego—and in exchange, bring to your mind, heart, and into your life the love of God and all His miraculous blessings. Your life will be one filled with good karma, the God-karma. By doing this you will bask in His love and light every day of your precious life. Always remember beloved souls, children of God, the Father, you can never escape karma, for karma is a major part of Universal Law, God's Law. Understand dear ones, if you steal, you will be stolen from. If you take from others, others will take from you. If you lie, you will be lied to. If you kill, you too shall be killed. On the other side of this, if you truly love (not lust), you shall be loved by many. If you give of yourself, you shall be given to in any hour of need. If you share your wealth, you will receive from God, the Father His wealth in the Kingdom of Heaven. *These statements are truth!*

Many here on the planet are going through lifetimes of karma and some are learning very difficult lessons through karma. We wish better for you. We wish for you to know and feel always in your life and heart God's infinite love for you. Unfortunately, many families do not feel this wonderful state of bliss. Instead, they feel pain and suffering, both emotional and physical, due to the effects of negative or bad karma. Understand, cherished ones of God, everything on this land is done by cause and effect, meaning there is an action and then a reaction. You have a thought-form in your mind which causes an action outward, which in turn causes a reaction back to you. If your thought-forms are of a good nature, the nature of God, then your action put outward is one of love and giving and the reaction back to you is one of great love and many blessings. The same is true for the negative side. If your thought-forms are ones of fear and anger, then your action presented outward is one of hatred and violence and the reaction back to you is even more violent and hate-based. The most powerful way to prevent the negative side from entering into your life, and therefore preventing negative karma, is by asking God, the Father, to purify your thoughts—all of your thoughts from the past to the present and into the future. Pray this prayer every day: *"Father, God in Heaven, I ask of you and give permission to you, to heal, cleanse and purify my mind and my thoughts from the past, present, and into the future. I ask you Father, God, for your enlightenment and your wisdom. I thank you for your love and blessings. Amen."* This prayer will bring to your life a cleansing, a purifying of your thought forms. Understand dear ones, God cannot do this unless you ASK Him to do so. God cannot and will not intervene into your lives, your hearts or your minds unless He is asked to do so through prayer. Prayer shows God your sincerity for Him to enter into your life and heart. Through prayer you open the door to God. The door to God is always and forever there and our Lord God, the Father is always waiting there behind it. However, beloved ones, *you* must open *your* door to God, for God will never force you to do anything. You always have free will and free choice. Through your free will and choice is how you find your true path to God. Understand, beloved children of God, the Father, the time to pray to God is NOW. Now is the time to end the cycle of bad karma, to put a stop to the negative side to this, the precious gift of life. Finding your way to God and keeping your connection with God strong is the only way to do this. Ask God to release from your mental and emotional bodies the negative emotions that keep you locked into fear and repeating the negative karma. Ask our God through prayer to clear from your minds thoughts of anger, fear, envy, prejudice, and ego. These are the emotions and feelings which keep you in the circle of fear, which in turn leads you into the cycle of negative karma.

Understand and know always, thought creates. Negative thoughts create negative actions and negative karma. Good thoughts, loving and positive thoughts, will always, without fail, create actions of kindness, love, and prosperity. This gives you the good karma, the God-karma, that keeps blessing you. This is really quite simple to know and understand, is it not?

This principle is also much easier to live by than you may think. Yes, you may have to let go of many feelings and emotions you have had with you, possibly for many years. Understand beloved ones, you are never too old nor is it ever too late to find God's loving peace in your heart. This is done easily through prayer—much prayer—every day prayer. This process and loving change is not done by only one prayer to God, the Father. You must be sincere and ask the Father daily for His purification and for the connection to be strong between God and you.

However, this glorious change can be achieved more rapidly if you were to take God's guidance and show some responsibility on your part by having a careful eye as to what television shows you watch. These television shows that portray violence and sexual encounters deem this an acceptable way to live in your society. This is absolutely *false truth!* God's universal laws are not written in the script of these violent movies and television shows. These acts of violence portrayed in these movies and television shows influence the mind and emotions of the people who watch them. This is TRUTH. The same applies for some of the music that is listened to by the people in your world. The music which tells disturbing tales of hatred and violence toward man and animal, can and does completely influence the mind and emotions of the people who listen to such music. These destructive negative forces breed hatred into the mind and heart which lead to violent acts. These destructive forces within the entertainment industry are the dark side working through the minds of people who write these movies, television shows, lyrics and sheet music that is of a violent content and negative music tones and lyrics. Remember, beloved ones of God, our Father, you always have free will and free choice. So you have the choice not to watch those movies and television shows, and to stop listening to the music which holds within it much negativity and harm. There are other types of movies and television shows that are of a loving nature and that are very educational to better one's self. There are many songs recorded by various people that express love and sing praise to the Lord our God. These songs will fill your heart with love and joy. *The choice is yours, beloved souls.* Your karma is your choice. Pray to the Father, God, every day. Ask our God to enter into your life and bring His love and purification into your mind and thoughts and center His love into your heart, so that you may know true love and peace in your life.

Call upon the Lord Jesus, Blessed Mother Mary, or myself (Saint Germain), or call upon the archangels—Archangel Michael or Archangel Gabriel, Archangel Uriel or Archangel Raphael—or any other Ascended Masters or angels of God you may know. Call upon us at any time or as many times as you may need or wish. We are always here for you and are very happy to help you. We are very pleased to hear from you. It is our pleasure to serve you. It is our want and divine pleasure to serve God. Call upon the Lord God, the Father, King of the Universe, and to the Ascended Masters and the archangels, for love, support, and guidance to make your karma the good karma—the God-karma—for blessings to yourself and your family and others. Blessed be the name of the Lord our God. My love is with you always.

Saint Germain,
received by Eve Barbieri

✢ Chapter 12 ✢

ANGELS

by
Mother Mary

✤ ANGELS ✤

This is Mary, mother of Jesus speaking. My love and blessings on all who are reading this.

Today we will concentrate on understanding the nature of angels. These most precious guardians are given to you out of the Father's great love. They also have free will and have chosen to serve the Light and bring God's love to each of you through their very own talents and areas of expertise. Yes, angels are not "jacks of all trades and masters of none." They are all experts in what they chose to do. Some are expert guardians. Others are experts in gardening. There are angels of love, angels of compassion, angels of finance, angels of the air, angels of fire, water angels and earth angels. There are angels of communication, and angels of relationships—even angels of nations, towns, and cities. There are angels of joy, angels of peace, and angels of forgiveness. There are angels who love to sing, those that love to dance, angel artists and poets. All that you see about you has been touched by angels. There are angels who work with animals, and you can call on them for help at any time with your pets. When you are confused, ask for an angel of clarity to show you the way. They bring God's love to you in every circumstance and it is their supreme joy to be of service to you and the Father in this way. They are eager to help and they learn from you, too. There are angels of the body to help you with its proper functioning. There are angels who love to cook and will help you prepare delicious, nourishing meals for yourself and your family.

Perhaps you may never have thought of them in this way, but begin to do so. There are angels of high technology, and those who enjoy building things with you. There are the problem solvers who will gather information for you.

Due to the Divine Edict of free will, it is necessary for you to ask and give permission for them to work with you. When you do, these gentle spirits will surround you with the tenderest love. They do not judge, ever. They cannot. It is not within their being to judge, and neither do they desire to do so. Their mission is to bring God's love into your life and to serve. You don't have to be in trouble to call on them. Some angels have chosen to be companions and just want to *be with you* when you are feeling alone.

So dear ones, enrich your life by entertaining these gentle beings in every area of your life, and teach your children these things. They are more open to receive this knowledge than many adults, and the blessing of these lessons will stay with them all their lives. Humans are creatures of habit and create many habits for themselves that are not always in their best interests. Create the habit of calling in the angels and working with them. This is a joyful habit that enhances life in all its aspects. When you write a letter, ask for an angel to write with you. Your letter will be a treasured gift to the recipient. If you have to give a talk, ask for an angel and your words will be profound. When you take a walk, ask an angel to go with you. You will notice things you never saw before. You will feel the breeze and the warmth of the sun in ways you never experienced.

The Father created a most beautiful world just for your pleasure, and gave you angels to guide, protect, and love you— and to show you how precious you are in His sight. Do not ignore these loving spirits; rather, seek them out. And one day you may feel their wings embracing you and their kiss upon your cheek. Open your God-eye and take note of Spirit around you. Open your heart to receive the love of God, for you are God's child and loved perfectly—no matter what. The angels of mercy are ever near and mercy is dispensed without measure. My Son said "judge (condemn) not." This means you are not to judge (condemn) yourself either. God does not. God only loves. Forgive. Forgive your mistakes. Forgive other's mistakes. Bless yourself. Bless each other. Bless God. Bless the angels. Bless the Earth and bless all creatures in all worlds. Bless the things you like and they will become more wonderful. Bless that which you do not like and you will begin to see it in a new way. It is easy to bless that which you love, but to bless that which irritates you is necessary in order to effect change for the better. As you work with the angels, your awareness of God will fill your life with wonder and miracles far beyond your expectations. You are loved without measure.

Mother Mary, mother of Jesus,
received by Romayne de Kanter

Chapter 13

THE HUMAN BIRTH PROCESS

by
Archangel Gabriel

✤ THE HUMAN BIRTH PROCESS ✤

Greetings and love from the angelic kingdom. This is Archangel Gabriel, and today I wish to give you some insight into the process of birth.

This is one of my assignments—to bring the beloved souls of God safely into the Earth plane. As you may remember, I was the one who brought the announcement of the birth of Jesus to Mother Mary. It was my great honor and mission to oversee the birth of the Divine One. I was also the "star" that guided the three wise men. All was fulfilled according to the Father's will.

Let me explain that birth is a rather complicated process, in that—in order for the plan to succeed—all events must be in place. You exist in the spirit world before birth and after death. There you meet with God and your guides and angels who have been assigned to you by the Father. You, together, decide on your next life lessons, and the experiences you will have. Other souls come into the picture to take their place in the plan. They agree to take part in your plan, and you in theirs. And so the stage is set, so to speak. You may think of it as perhaps the making of a movie. There are many parallels in the Earth plane and the spiritual dimensions. In a very real sense, you bring these ideas—the movies, plays, and other forms of entertainment—from the spirit world and duplicate them on Earth in an attempt to remind you of what is truly real on a deeper soul level. The term "as above, so below" is a truth, in that it parallels life in your world. In the spirit world you have a spiritual family to love and support you, you have friends, you have pets, and you have school and work. You do not "float around heaven all day." You are very busy. There are games, parties, and entertainments of various forms. Talent does not cease with death. It remains with you and is much enhanced. As an example, if perhaps you are an artist, your paintings in the spirit world are far more glorious, with incredible colors not known on Earth. So the "routine" of life in both worlds is much the same.

Now, beloved souls, the play begins. At the proper time in the script, you make your entrance and the birth occurs. Let me explain that you, as a spirit soul, still have free will. The same is true for those now in the physical Earth plane. This is where events sometimes go wrong. If some soul in the "play" or event forgets their role and deviates from the plot, this throws the timing off, so to speak, and your scheduled entrance, or birth, may be pushed forward, delayed, or eliminated completely. To avoid this, it is the job of the angels and guides of each of you to do all they can to keep the plot intact without interfering with your free will. This is a tall order for these beings who work with you, and their job is not an easy one. If, for instance, the timing is wrong, there may well be an interruption in the birth process, known to you as a miscarriage. This is not to say that you have lost your chance at birthing. But you have chosen to be born at a later time when it would be more advantageous for your life purpose. A decision of this kind is made and agreed upon with God in the spirit world.

Let me impress upon you the importance of your Earth experience. The Father takes this very seriously. The opportunities for spiritual growth while in the Earth plane are tremendous. It is a marvelous opportunity to advance rapidly in spirit. By your choices, you either gain or lose ground. Either way, it is a learning tool like no other. Therefore, the planet Earth is very dear to the Father's heart, and He has designed it perfectly for your enjoyment. Wonderful angels and nature spirits care for everything and fill it with the Father's love. It is all for you, dear children of God, to facilitate your growth in spirit.

Your agreement with God in this lifetime and all lifetimes on Earth is a sacred one. It is a type of contract of the highest order. It is not "written in stone," but it is written in your Book of Life and recorded there. It is more permanent than stone. In your world, if you break a contract, you are often taken before a judge in a court of law and assessed fines and penalties. So it is in the spirit world. To break a sacred contract is a serious thing, with consequences and penalties. This was fully explained and understood by you, as you placed your seal upon it.

It is understood that you do not consciously remember this contract that you are in the process of fulfilling. But your soul knows, as do your guides and angels. They will always lead you on the right path. If you are unsure about your choices—if you are confused—the Father will always point the way. So prayer is good. Pray always for things to be done in Divine Order. Then all will fall into place as it should. The Father will never leave you, nor forsake you. That is His part of this sacred contract. If you yield to God, you cannot lose.

To those of God's children about to give birth, let me congratulate you and extend all manner of blessings to you. There are many angels who oversee the entire birthing process and will be happy to assist you with your concerns before, during, and after the birth of the child. You need only ask. It is one of the greatest joys of your life, and we rejoice with each of you. Each God-child is so very precious in the miracle of life.

Your gift to each other in the form of mutual love and support in the quest for spiritual perfection is a source of joy to God, and great are your rewards.

I, Archangel Gabriel, am watching over each of you on your Earth journey, and extend God's blessings to all.

Archangel Gabriel,
received by Romayne de Kanter

CHAPTER 14

DEATH AND THE AFTERLIFE

by
Saint Germain

✤ DEATH AND THE AFTERLIFE ✤

Greetings and great love to all. This is Saint Germain. Today I wish to speak to you about a very popular topic on the Earth plane. I wish to speak to you about what you call death. As you may know already, no one really dies. You simply leave your physical body and return to the spirit plane. Everyone is spirit. Before you are a human being, you are a spirit being. A spirit being looks very much the same as a human being. However, the spirit is much brighter and has a glow of light around them and inside of them. The only time there is a very dim glow is when a spirit has the dark side (the dark beings) around them. Whether you have a bright glow of God's Love all around and through you, or a dim or gray glow will depend on how you lived your life on Earth. Your physical actions and/or mental thoughts will either bring light into your soul, or keep the light of your soul dim.

PART 1:

WHAT HAPPENS WHEN YOU DIE

Many times the spirit will leave the body before the death of the physical body has occurred. This may happen during a tragic death, such as an airplane crash, automobile accident, earthquake, drowning, or anytime the death is sudden or imminent. What will happen is that the life force—your spirit—will leave the body, but stay near the physical body. This is so you will understand that *your physical death has taken place.* You can remain with your physical body for a time, if you wish, in order to say goodbye to it. But it is necessary to leave it behind after a short time. The spirit needs to move on. It is not healthy for a spirit to linger on the Earth plane for an extended period of time.

Now, it is important to make clear—every spirit being knows their physical death has taken place. This is true even if the physical body is no longer intact (complete). For example, if the physical body was dismembered because of a violent act, an airplane crash, a fire, etc. , then that human being/spirit being's angel will inform the spirit being of their physical death. May I, Saint Germain, state here and now, every human being on the Earth plane has at least one angel of God assigned to be with them at all times. This angel never leaves or abandons the person at any time—even after the person's physical death. One of the many glorious assignments of God's angels is to give love, guidance, and understanding to the people of Earth. Whether or not a spirit being wishes to accept their physical death is another matter. Some spirit beings wish to stay Earth-bound. I will speak more on this subject a little later in this chapter.

Understand, dear ones, every spirit has a life to live in the spirit plane—a life to return to. When a spirit leaves the body, they are *never alone. No person dies alone, ever!* There is always Divine guidance back to the spirit plane, unless that person had committed (in this life) terrible crimes and great sins against God and all of God's Creation. That person too, is not alone. However, their return is somewhat different. I will reflect upon that a little later, as well. But for the people who lived a decent life, one of mostly joy and love, then those people will be divinely guided by God's angels and their spirit guides to go into the Light. For some, they may be led by their angels and guides over to a vortex of white light that shines down from the heavens while they are still on the Earth. This vortex leads them into a tunnel. For others, they may (soon after seeing their deceased physical body) go swiftly into a tunnel. This is the true "tunnel of love." For most people, they will see bright, beautiful light at the end of this tunnel. While traveling through the tunnel they will feel love and great comfort. This is God's light that they see and God's love that they feel.

Upon entering the Light after going through the tunnel, the spirit being will be greeted by Saint Peter and/or other angels and guides who help the others into the Light. At this time, the spirit being will be led into to a beautiful garden, or to a room that is designed to make the spirit feel very comfortable and at home. Then the Heavenly Father will put a screen of light before the spirit being. On this screen, the spirit being will see his/her entire life review. The spirit being will be shown their Earth life in great detail, from infancy to the age they were when they passed away. This life review is much like a film about the spirit being's Earth life and all the spirit being did, every action, good or bad. The spirit will somewhat relive that Earth life; however, it will not take nearly as long. Understand, there is no concept of third-dimensional time in the spirit plane. There is no linear time. This spirit being will feel every emotion they have given out to others.

Allow me to explain. The spirit being will feel every emotion of joy, happiness, love and kindness that his or her actions are responsible for, and the spirit will also feel all the pain, sorrow, and hatred that their actions caused others to feel. The spirit being will be shown every experience of love given by them to other people, and that spirit being will also be shown every experience of hatred and pain given by them to others. The spirit being will be given information on how each experience, whether good or bad, affected the lives of the other people. The spirit being will know how the joyous things he or she did changed for the better all the lives of all the people affected by those wonderful acts. And they will also know how the acts he or she had done out of hatred and fear caused the lives of those affected to change for the worse. The spirit being's angels and spirit guides will be there to help and assist the spirit, as this is a very emotional time.

After things have settled a bit, the spirit being will be greeted by the Angels of the Akashic Records (The Planetary Life Records) and that spirit being will receive from them their past Earth Life Contract. This contract was written by God and the spirit being before that incarnation into the Earth life took place. At this time, the spirit will know if he or she accomplished all that the spirit set out to do on the Earth plane in that past life. What the spirit being accomplished according to what was written in the contract will be written in the spirit's Akashic Record. What was not accomplished in the Earth life will be put into a file (as you would say), and placed in the area of the Universe where the life contracts are discussed and signed by the spirit being. This file will lay dormant until the spirit being wishes to incarnate again.

Understand, beloved souls, the spirit being's Earth life review, and the spirit being's Akashic Record discussion are a time of private counsel. This is a time of great understanding and knowledge given for the spirit to completely understand and know, without question, that all of the wrong things they have done were sins against God, themselves, and others. This is so the spirit being will have a total understanding of what evil is and how evil deeds affect themselves, the people of the world, the planet Earth, and God, the Father. The spirit being will also know and understand how love—all types of love given: a smile, a good thought, a kind and generous act, and prayers to God—affects themselves, the people of the world, the planet, and God, the Father. Every spirit being who wishes to join God and other spirits in the spirit plane, and before they choose to incarnate into a physical life again, must first go through this process to see, feel, and understand their past life review and discuss this with God and the Lord Jesus. The spirit being must also discuss their Akashic Record (their past lives record) with God, the Lord Jesus, and the Angels of the Planetary Life Records. There are no exceptions to this strictly enforced Universal Law.

Now, at this point, many different things may happen for the spirit being, depending on various factors. The spirit being will usually meet up with relatives and friends who are also in spirit. Spirit beings can meet up with the past spirit relatives and spirit friends when they have just arrived into the Light. However, it is not likely that spirit friends and spirit relatives are present during the time of spiritual business—the past life review and Akashic Record discussion. These are usually done in a more private manner, involving God, Jesus, angels and some spirit guides.

Now, if (before the physical death) the person was very ill, that spirit being may want to take a rest and receive much healing. However, most of the spirits who cross over into the spirit plane like to "pop" back to Earth, so to speak, and be with family and friends during their funeral. That is why, when you are at the funeral of a departed person, you may "feel" their presence in the room. That is because they are there! The spirit usually does not stay too long after all the ceremonies. They can come and visit from time to time. However, most—almost all—spirits who have departed from a physical life do not make their dwellings on the Earth plane. In order to lead a happier life, they must make their homes back in the spirit plane.

PART 2:

THE HEALING

As I have said, some spirit beings may need rest and healing. There are angels who are termed *The Healing Angels—The Lightbearers.* Usually these angels will lead the spirit being who is in need of rest and healing to the place called *The Love Healing Center.* This is a beautiful palace in the spirit plane, and the feeling of this great place is one of comfort and love. God, the Father, forever dwells in this place along with The Healing Angels—The Lightbearers (the bringers of God's healing light), and the spirit being patients. The Lord Jesus, Mother Mary, other Ascended Masters, along with the archangels and God's angels will visit this place frequently to see how every spirit is doing. *All healing is done through God's almighty powerful love in this place in the universe.* That is all that is ever needed. All healing—true healing—is only done through God's love. These Healing Angels—The Lightbearers, have God's healing love and light shine through them and into the soul of the spirit being. This will go on for as long as needed for the spirit being to be Divinely healed completely. Understand, beloved ones, your soul is the core of your being. In your soul is where the most pain and trauma is held. God's love heals all, and after the spirit being is divinely healed, he or she can stay in The Love Healing Center and rest for as long as they wish. Or if they want, they can return to the place where the spirit beings make their homes and begin their work in spirit.

PART 3:

SPIRIT BEINGS ARE VERY MUCH ALIVE

I, Saint Germain, wish for you to please understand this and know this in your heart. Spirit beings are just as alive as you are. Actually, they are more alive because they are not in a third-dimensional body. Their spirit body is energy from God, our Creator. God's energy is everlasting, infinite, and ever powerful—always.

(Just a note: There are no sexual relations done in the spirit plane. Sex is a physical body desire due to certain changes in hormones within the physical body. Spirit beings do not possess physical body hormones. However, spirit beings do share loving experiences. Love in the spirit world is a reciprocal process. Spirit beings give love from their being and soul and receive love in return. These love exchanges are very fulfilling and pure in the eyes of God.)

Spirit beings have all the five senses and more. Spirits can see, hear, touch, taste, smell, feel—both emotionally and with their spirit bodies—and speak and understand others. Spirit beings can walk, run, sing, and dance. They can feel a breeze. Spirits can feel the warm sun and the gentle droplets of rain. Spirit beings can also see, smell, touch, and feel the beautiful flowers that are so bountiful in the lovely fields of the spirit plane. However, there is no skin color of the spirit being. They are all one color, which is the color of God's light. The only time this will change is when they are told someone they know from the Earth plane is returning to spirit. Then that spirit being, through thought, will change their appearance to what that person remembers them to look like before they passed away.

This is why people who have had near death experiences will see their dead grandmother or their dead parents, who look just like they remember. This is done so that the spirit being who has just returned to the spirit plane will quickly recognize their spirit friends and spirit relatives. This helps the spirit being who has just returned to feel more relaxed and comforted, since there is quite a bit of adjusting to do already.

Most spirit beings will look very similar to the way they did in their Earth life when they were about the age of 25 years old. Most spirit beings will actually choose and keep this appearance. Now if a child or teenager crosses over into the spirit plane (dies), they will usually finish maturing there. The children usually return to the spirit plane the same age as they were when they "died," and, depending on their age, will mature at the pace they choose. I will give information on children in the spirit plane in this chapter. Understand beloved souls, a spirit being is who you truly are. You are a human being and a spirit being, and you will live for all eternity. All spirit beings, and all beings of God, will live **forever!** At times this may be difficult to conceive because you cannot see or hear your loved ones who have returned back to the spirit world. Please, beloved ones, rest assured your departed loved ones are very much alive and always will be.

PART 4

CHILDREN IN THE SPIRIT PLANE

Greetings. I, Saint Germain have been asked by the oracles of this book to reflect on the children and family pets in the spirit plane. I will begin by talking about the children in the spirit world. As I have said before, and will say again, every human being who has taken a breath on Earth will have a life review and Akashic (past life) Record discussion. This is for the purpose of understanding and recording the past Earth life, no matter how short in time the past life was. You see, beloved ones, some spirit beings choose to come into a short Earth life for a specific experience. For example, some spirit beings come into the physical life to experience an infantile disease, or to be abused and killed as an infant for the purpose of teaching their loved ones on Earth to forgive by finding their own spiritual path to God. (You must understand, the only way to truly forgive another is by holding the Light of God in your heart). Or it is possible the spirit being, while in the spirit plane, chose to come into an Earth life to be abused and killed as an infant to rectify their past karma.

This is why, as I have said before, "Judge not"—you are not to judge God or any person, for you do not know anyone's Earth life plan. If an infant dies on the Earth plane, that young child's spirit will be cared for by either family spirit beings associated with the Earth plane family, or by other loving spirit families who wish to give their love and attention to this young child's spirit. If a young child died violently or tragically and has a difficult time adjusting to the fact that they have returned to spirit, or if they miss their parents and close friends, there is much support and love given to them. There are highly evolved spirit beings along with the Angels of Counsel who give assistance to these spirit being children who, at times, will feel distress. These spirit counselors give these spirit being children much love and healing from God, the Father. This healing and love counseling is endless and they are at the spirit child's service anytime, for as long as the spirit being child is in need. All children in the spirit world are protected and cherished by God and His forces of light.

As you know, the human being has different stages of development: infant, adolescent, adult, and elderly. In regards to the spirit being, the development is somewhat different. The spirit body can progress through these different stages without the physical deterioration that exists on Earth. Every spirit being who comes into the light of the spirit plane is able to fully understand they have crossed over into the Heavens, no matter how young the child was when he or she "died." You must always remember, beloved ones, your children are also God's children. God never abandons any of His Creation. When a child "dies," whatever the age, there are legions of angels waiting on the other side, the spirit plane, to give love and assistance. The Lord Jesus greets every child spirit and showers the child spirit being with love, healing, and understanding.

This young child spirit being receives (in a delicate manner) their life review and their Akashic (past life) Record discussion. The child spirit being then can mature or develop in a gradual manner if they so wish. Since there is no timetable in the spirit world, this development of a child spirit being into a more mature spirit being (about the age of 25 Earth years) will depend on the individualism of that spirit. For example, some child spirit beings wish to mature more quickly, while other child spirits wish to mature in a more gradual mode. They wish to extend their childlike and playful demeanor. This allows more of a variety of spirit beings in the spirit world. Beloved souls, always know in your hearts and minds, God, our Father, loves every human being and every spirit being (as they are one and the same), no matter the age. Every one of His children is loved, cherished, and perfectly cared for in the spirit plane.

PART 5:

PETS

We in the spirit plane understand there are some people who are curious and wonder about the animals when they "die," especially the beloved family pets. Just as human beings do not die, neither do animal beings. None—not any of God's Creation dies. All of God's Creation is a part of God and a part of God's love energy. God's energy lives forever. So, in regard to the animals who leave the Earth plane and cross over into the spirit world, they are very much alive. They simply leave one dimension and go into another.

There are many aspects or realms of the spirit world. One is the animal kingdom. This is where the animals who lived on Earth dwell when they die their physical death. There are the "wild" animals in the animal kingdom, as well as animals who lived with man in a domestic way—for example, dogs, cats, horses, and birds, to name a few. However, I wish to make understood, "wild" animals are not dangerous in any way in the animal kingdom. Those particular instincts for survival are located only in the *physical* animal's body. Survival is a characteristic of the third dimension. It is not necessary in the spirit world. All animal spirit beings, large and small, live together in total and complete harmony in the animal kingdom.

Now, concerning your family pets, every animal has a spirit body—one that is easily recognized and known by the spirit being who knew that animal while they were both in physical bodies on the Earth plane. In easier words, if you have had a family pet with whom you lived, you will be able to see and love again that same pet in the spirit plane. There are many loving animal spirit beings who live with spirit being families in the spirit plane. However, the pet may take on a somewhat different appearance than the physical body it had while on Earth. As there are no old or elderly spirit beings, the same is true for animal spirit beings. All animal spirits are in the stage that is considered to be their prime age during their Earth life. However, their spirit bodies may look a bit different than what their Earth life physical bodies looked like. Understand though, all spirit beings will recognize their pets that are in spirit when in the spirit plane. A dog will still be a dog. A cat will be a cat, and so on. They will simply take on a more glowing animal appearance. The animal spirit will still possess all those wonderful, playful, happy and loving characteristics of their personality while on Earth. However, any of the negative traits they carried on Earth will be diminished. The animal spirit returns to its true loving form in the spirit plane and animal kingdom in the spirit world. Just as animals bring love, enlightenment, and joy to the people of Earth and also to the planet Earth herself, the same is true in the spirit world. Animals bring much love, happiness, and uplifting energy to the spirit world. All animals, both in the physical form and spirit form, are one of God's truly miraculous gifts to all the universe.

PART 6

A DESCRIPTION OF THE SPIRIT WORLD

Greetings once again. This is Saint Germain. In this brief part of this chapter on physical death and the afterlife, I wish to give you a general description of the spirit world. I will start by saying it is much like the planet Earth. However, there is no pollution in the spirit world of *any* kind—only true scenic beauty possessing all its majesty from the Creator of all, The Lord, our God. The spirit world is beautiful in its landscapes of rushing waterfalls, clear, flowing rivers, and oceans of great marvel, with sand that contains all the colors of the rainbow. Also in the spirit world are mountains of great, wondrous magnitude with beauty so monumental that any worded description gives little justice. As the mountains of Earth hold the greatest and most powerful energy known to mankind, the same is true in the spirit world. These mountains of fabulous mystic majesty have within them some of the most powerful God-energy in the universe.

In addition to these wonders, the spirit world contains lush greenery, grass that flows in the wind with vibrant colors, and endless fields of beautiful flowers. A vast variety of trees and forests full of towering pine trees of all kinds grace the land. Canyons with layers of rock that project color rays from every Ascended Master, which give love, healing, and enlightenment to all who visit. Deserts so rich in beauty with majestic views and towering rock monuments hail to the heavens. The skies are filled with clouds of endless entertainment for the spirit being's eye to behold. The night skies are filled with bright shimmering stars that sparkle and gleam greater than any diamonds. And in the spirit world is an open sky where spirits can see all the planets (including Earth) of this wonderful galaxy. These are just some of the marvelous scenic wonders of the spirit world. And as the popular phrase goes, this is just "the tip of the iceberg" (and yes, the spirit world has those, too). The momentous beauty of the spirit world is indeed challenging to put into a vocabulary. The monumental wonders of the spirit world are too numerous to mention. This grand scale of beauty and majesty of love is both infinite and ever-changing in the spirit world, for God, our Creator and Father in Heaven, is forever giving His love and powerful energy to all worlds and all His Creation.

PART 7

EVERYTHING IS THOUGHT

As you know in your world, planet Earth, thought is the first step for man to create. Then mankind must work the third-dimensional laws of physics to create a manifestation from that single thought. This is a universal third-dimensional law. This law from God serves the growth and evolvement of mankind. This particular law does not apply in the spirit plane.

As you know, spirit beings no longer live in a third-dimensional physical body. In other words, their spirit self is not encased by a third-dimensional embodiment, unless that spirit being incarnates to Earth again. Because of this, spirit beings create almost instantaneously with thought. And what spirit beings create with their thoughts are very real manifestations in the spirit plane. They can create very nice homes, food, music, furniture to sit and lie on, and they can teleport wherever they want or need to be. The spirit beings will think of a certain place and they will be there. This is called *Teleporting*. This is how a spirit being travels. Understand, beloved ones, all God's Creation is energy—love energy. So you see, spirit beings are energy too. When a spirit being thinks of themselves in a certain place, they create a concentrated thought form that focuses their energy (which is themselves, since they *are* energy) into that place. This places the spirit being in a different place through their thought. (Just a note: Human beings have the capacity to do this in their minds; however, they have not yet evolved their minds and brains for teleporting to take place. This is why you, as humans, must use other means of transportation if you wish to travel to a different destination.)

Spirit beings communicate differently than human beings. Spirit beings can speak to one another and they can also communicate telepathically. As I have said, spirits can sing. And some spirits sing beautiful love songs about the heavens and all the wonders of God. Spirits' voices are somewhat different than humans' voices. As with human beings, spirits also use certain tones to create and form words for the use of expression. However, the spirit tones are somewhat higher, which in turn will make the spirit voice sound higher than a human voice. Clearly, there are no telephones in the spirit world. Because of this, spirit beings can communicate their thoughts to one another (regardless of the distance) through the transmitting energy method known as telepathy. When spirits communicate telepathically, they must first visualize the spirit being they wish to send messages to. Then the spirits focus their thought forms to another spirit or spirits to whom they are wanting to communicate with. This transfer of energy thought-forms from one spirit mind to another spirit mind or to a group of spirits' minds is telepathy. This is how spirit beings communicate long distance (or any distance) in the spirit world.

All thoughts create. On the Earth plane, all the thoughts you have, every thought of every day, will map out your destiny. Where you are in your life, the path you are on, is due to every thought you have had in your entire life. Thoughts are very powerful. This is because you give *your* power to these thoughts. Good thoughts will create good for you and always bring to you a positive outcome to any circumstance. The same is true for bad or negative thoughts. Your negative thoughts will generate harm to you and will make every situation ugly and tainted. This same principle applies in the spirit plane. The spirit beings who have only kind and loving and positive thoughts will live a very joyous and happy life as a spirit being and will be surrounded by those spirit beings who have those same loving thought-forms. However, the spirit beings who have negative thoughts, who think of evil, failure, and pain, will live their spirit life in much the same way because their thoughts created this for them. They will live a life of pain, suffering, hatred, and sorrow. So, beloved children of God, take the time to think about your thoughts—for to change a negative thought to a positive thought will always change your life and the lives of those close to you for the better. My Violet Flame of purity and love is offered to all.

PART 8:

HOME AND WORK

I, Saint Germain will reflect upon some of the glorious activities spirit beings can do in the spirit plane and beyond. You see, every spirit being does something, and every spirit being is placed in a certain area of the spirit plane or spirit world according to their spiritual evolvement. The degree of spiritual evolvement is determined by the amount of light that is held within the soul. Most spirit beings will create for themselves a home or return to the home they had before they came into the past Earth-life incarnation. This is done, as I have said earlier, after the Earth-life review, the Akashic Record discussion and healing (if needed).

Understand, another word for spirit being is Light body. The Light body (spirit being) is made up of Love/Light energy from God. Some spirit beings hold more light than other spirit beings. Understand beloved ones, spirit beings or Light bodies do not require the same necessities that physical bodies do to maintain their survival. Spirit beings, or Light bodies do not have a need for food, shelter, or clothing. These are created by the spirit being out of want, not need. The health of a spirit being or Light body depends on the amount of love they possess in their soul. The more the love, the brighter the light, the healthier the spirit being, and of course, the opposite of this is true as well. Spirit beings will create food, shelter, and clothing for the purposes of celebrations, ceremonies, or because of habit.

All spirit beings have a job to do. There are no television sets in the spirit plane, so therefore there are no couch potatoes. There is much to do there. As the people of the planet Earth have an enormous network of numerous systems, all inter-related, so does the spirit plane. Only this is God's networking, which means it is much more peaceful and not chaotic at any time.

It is important to mention, as people on the Earth plane have various social and religious groups of people, so does the spirit plane. These various types of group settings are determined by the amount of light a spirit being holds within their body (their spirit body). All spirit beings who may want to carry more light into their bodies are offered much love and healing from not only The Healing Angels—The Lightbearers, but also God's elite Angels of Light. These angels are very powerful and live on a very high vibration.

There is much spiritual work done by spirit beings in the spirit plane. Some spirit beings work with the people of Earth. For example, some of the more highly evolved spirit beings will help mankind with different projects for the betterment of human beings, such as vaccines to prevent harmful illnesses. And mankind had much assistance in the understanding of the crystal to form the computer chip. Also, there are spirit beings who will guide the people of Earth to live their life in a more positive way. This is done if the people have prayed to God and have much faith. I must make clear, these spirit beings who help mankind in positive ways and work for the benefit of humanity hold an enormous amount of light in their spirit body. And there are some spirit beings who work in the spirit plane, doing such things as planning festivals and teaching children spirits and other spirit beings about God and His very powerful, unconditional love. There are no traffic jams in the spirit plane. There are no crimes committed in the spirit plane. There are no fights or pain done to others there. This is a place of peace, love, and joy.

PART 9

TRAVEL

Now there are some spirit beings who wish to travel. Traveling in the spirit form is much easier and more enjoyable than in the human form. As I have mentioned earlier, spirit beings travel by teleporting. Teleporting can be done basically in two ways, instantaneous and gradual. Gradual teleporting is done at a slower pace or calmer speed where the spirit being can take in all the beauty and wonders of where they are traveling. As you may say, there are many roses to smell along the way. There are numerous places in this universe that are of the most majestic beauty you could ever imagine. God, the Father, creates only love and pure beauty.

For example, there is a place called the Crystal Cities. These beautiful, majestic cities make up a wonderful world beyond what the human mind can ever imagine. There is also a place called "The City of God's Love for All." In this place, all who visit are given a beautiful crystal, stone, or a trinket as a remembrance of this beautiful City of Love. The spirit being brings this love object back with them to their homes and this crystal, stone, or trinket will radiate love inside of that home and to all spirit beings who dwell there. These are just a couple of the beautiful places of great love and purity that exist in this universe. The wonderful places of God's love and majestic beauty are too numerous to mention them all.

Some spirit beings also will take short trips to the Earth plane. Most people of Earth will not see them, but will sometimes feel a wonderful sensation around them or people will feel their hair touched or their arm or face touched. These are spirit beings letting you know they are visiting you. Or at times you may even have a wonderful memory of you and them together. This is the spirit being giving you this thought-form while they are visiting you. Now it is important to make very clear, spirit beings do not stay for very long. Spirit beings can visit the Earth for a short time only. They must return to the spirit plane to live their lives as a spirit there (unless the spirit is an Earth-bound spirit, in which case this spirit being has not yet crossed over into the light and into the spirit plane).

PART 10:

THE DARK SIDE

I, Saint Germain, will now speak to you about the other side of Light—the Dark World. As you know, free will and free choice is given to you, human beings, by God, the Father. This is also true for spirit beings. There are some spirit beings who wish to serve the dark forces. These dark spirit beings have not crossed over into the Light and into the spirit plane to receive their life review and Akashic record discussion, and will not be allowed into another Earth incarnation until they have done so. However, please understand this, these dark spirit beings can and do attach themselves to a human being's energy field— their aura. This is done by the person's own will—not God's will. The dark spirit beings come into a person's energy field through the person's own actions, through the seven deadly sins. The seven deadly sins are sloth, greed, hatred, lust, gluttony, pride, and envy. These sins are termed *deadly* because when people possess these harmful mental and emotional thoughts, they breed fear into mankind's hearts and lives which greatly weakens their connection to God, the Father, which in turn allows the dark side to come in and destroy. This is why all the Ascended Masters and archangels who have come through these two beloved oracles have said repeatedly to pray to God daily—twice daily—for a strong connection to God, our powerful loving Father, Creator of all universes and all worlds. The purpose of this book is to make understood to all who read this that the stronger your connection to God is, the more complete your life will be, both here on the Earth plane as a human being, and as a spirit being. The stronger your connection to God, the Father, the more God's Light is surrounding you at all times to give you love and protection from all harm. The dark spirit beings do exist. However, they have no power against the Light of God. The only power the dark spirit beings have is the power *you* give them. This is done when you are in fear. Whenever you feel fear, the first thing to do is pray to God for Light, and the Christ Light to be above you, below you, to the left of you, to the right of you, all around you and through you. (Do you see how that pattern makes the symbol of the cross with a circle around it?) The second thing to do is BREATHE. Breathe deeply—several times. This allows your aura, your energy field, to be expanded and empowered by the Light of God.

When you feel you need protection, call upon God and the Archangel Michael to send protection to you. This protection, the White Light of God and the shield from all danger and harm from the Archangel Michael, will be sent to you immediately. The dark side, the dark beings, cannot harm you IF you ask God, the Father, for protection. Understand beloved souls, you must ASK for your protection and for the protection of your family before you can be saved from the harmful destruction these dark beings can do.

It is obvious that throughout time and in your world today there are many human beings that have chosen the path of darkness. They have chosen a path away from God, the Father. There are many reasons why some human beings have chosen to serve the dark side. I will say here and now, the easiest way for a dark spirit being to attach themselves to your energy field—your aura—is by the disconnecting of your God-mind. One way this is done is by the use of alcohol and mind-altering drugs. You see, beloved souls, when a person drinks excessively or takes drugs that alter the mind, that in turn alters the stability of the mind. Then that person has disconnected that part of their brain that brings their God-mind into their consciousness. This temporary disconnect of the God-mind separates them from God for the amount of time they are under the influence of the alcohol or drugs.

It is during this temporary disconnect from the God-mind and the separation from God, that the dark spirit beings will come into a person's energy field (aura). Needless to say, the night-clubs and taverns around the world have many, many dark spirit beings waiting to invade people's energy fields. And it is important to make clear that there are some dark spirit beings that refuse to leave a person's energy field—their aura—after the person has returned to a normal state of mind. What I, Saint Germain, am saying is: these dark spirits can stay with a person for many years, feeding off the person's fear. These dark spirits can and do cause much destruction in people's lives. They, the dark spirits that attach themselves to people's energy field, can cause illness and suffering. This is one reason why gluttony is one of the seven deadly sins. Gluttony, which includes drunkenness and drug abuse, is one way that a person's connection to God is weakened greatly. This is why our God, the Father, holds these sins contemptible in His heart. These sins cause His children great pain and suffering.

There are other ways the dark spirit beings can attach them-selves and invade a person's energy field. That is if the person holds hatred, prejudice, and judgment in their hearts, minds, and in their lives. These harmful emotions cause a person to be disconnected from their God-mind, thereby separating them from God by their own thoughts. Understand, beloved souls, hatred, prejudice, judgment, and anger are the opposite of our loving God. God is, at all times, love, peace, joy, kindness, and giving to all. You see beloved souls, anger, hatred, prejudice, and judgment of others are emotions that are generated by fear. The dark spirit beings take a person's fear and use that as their power. The dark spirit beings then manipulate that power (fear) given to them by the person, by turning it into a stronger, more gripping fear. Understand, beloved souls of God, fear is energy, just as love is energy. Your energy can be either one of fear or one of love. If you choose love for your personal energy, then you must turn to God, for God is the only and most powerful source of love.

It is important for you to understand that the dark spirit beings will use a person's energy through that person's fear to impose their will—the dark will—on the person's life. This cannot and will not happen if you have a strong connection with God, the Loving Father in Heaven. These dark spirit beings live in the fourth dimension. They live in the lower astral plane or realm, as it is often termed. In the astral realm there are two different levels—the lower astral realm (this is called The Dark World), and the higher astral realm. The higher astral realm is where some more "normal" spirit beings dwell as well as some spirit guides that many of the psychics today will get much of their information from. After the higher astral realm is the etheric realm. This is where many of the more advanced and evolved spirit beings will live.

The lower astral realm—The Dark World, as it is also termed—is a very dense place that has a very low vibration—a low frequency. The dark spirit beings are stuck in this place of great misery unless they call out to the Father God or the Lord Jesus Christ for salvation. This is the only way out of the lower astral realm. The lower astral realm is not the spirit plane. The spirit plane is in the higher astral realm and the etheric realm. The lower astral realm could be termed as Hell. When a dark spirit being wishes to leave that horrible place, they (as I have said before) must call out to the Father, God, or The Lord Jesus Christ, to be saved. Then the dark spirit will be taken to an area called The Gray Zone, where, while heavily guarded, the dark spirit will receive his or her life review and Akashic Record discussion. After that is completed, God's powerful angels will evaluate the dark spirit's mindset.

If that dark spirit sincerely feels sorrow and remorse for what they have done, and wish to rectify the evil they have done, then they will be guided to a special area to receive healing and education about crimes and sins and how it affects God and the people of Earth. The dark spirit will also be taught about God's love and its effects on the people of the Earth. Then that more enlightened spirit being will be placed in an area of the spirit plane according to the amount of light that the spirit being holds within its spirit body and its soul. Now, I must make this understood. It is not possible in any way for a dark spirit being or any spirit being or any person to lie to God about their feelings or thoughts. God, the Father, created every spirit being and every human being. Therefore God knows every deep silent thought and *every* thought in every being's mind.

If, after receiving their life review and Akashic Record discussion, the dark spirit being feels no sorrow, no remorse, for the evil they have done, then that dark spirit will be taken to a place where they *cannot* do any harm. This is a place of total rest. This dark spirit being will be placed in a state known as "suspended animation." In this state, the dark spirit's energy is inert, completely inactive. The dark spirit being is at rest. It can be termed in your language that this dark spirit is kept in a sleep state. During this time, this spirit being is receiving much healing and much love from God. Understand, beloved souls, these dark spirit beings are also children of God and He loves them as He loves all His children. The dark spirit beings have lost their way from God, our Father. You see, beloved souls, God and all His forces of Light want every one of God's children to be back in the loving arms of God, our Father. And much love energy is put forth from God and His elite forces of Light so that all of God's children can find the path back to God. So if they wish, they can be with God and live in His light and His love again.

Now, this spirit being in the state of suspended animation is not forgotten. As I have said, this spirit receives much healing and love from God. Then this spirit being is periodically awakened into full consciousness and their mindset is evaluated again by God's powerful angels. If this spirit being does not sincerely feel sorrow, remorse, and the wish to rectify the evil they have done, then that spirit being will then return to the state of suspended animation for another period of rest and receive more healing and love. This may go on for eons, for some dark spirit beings refuse to awaken themselves into the light and love of God. If this dark spirit *does* feel sincere sorrow and remorse, and wishes to rectify the evil they have done, and bring love to the pain and suffering they have caused during that human being's life incarnation, then they will be brought to the special place of education and healing. After this, these more enlightened spirit beings can continue their advancement in the light of God, if it is their wish to do so.

PART II:

EARTH-BOUND SPIRITS

Yes, beloved souls, there is such a thing as ghosts. These are actually termed Earth-bound spirits. These spirits refuse to accept the fact that they are dead—well, may I say, their physical body has ceased its functions. Everyone is spirit. No one ever dies; they simply leave one dimension and cross over into another. However, Earth-bound spirits wish to stay on the Earth plane. They do not wish to move on.

It is important I make this absolutely clear. Every human being who dies *knows* their physical death has occurred. This is without fail, even if, as I have said earlier in this chapter, their physical body is not recognized by the spirit being. Every human being has at least one angel assigned to be with them at all times—even the human beings who serve darkness (although their angels are at a distance from them due to the human being's own desire). At the time of physical death, their angel will tell them—every spirit being—so they absolutely understand that they have died. Some spirit beings will not want to accept this fact and will continue to stay Earth-bound. May I say here and now, this is a waste, a very bleak state for these spirit beings to be in. Earth-bound spirit beings cannot incarnate again until they have moved on to the spirit plane and have had their life review and Akashic Record discussion. What this means is that this Earth-bound spirit being is stuck in between worlds, by their own will.

This is truly a sad time. During the course of this stay on the Earth plane, many attempts are made by God and His angels and the spirit being's spirit guides to bring these spirits back to the spirit plane. The Tunnel of Light, the vortex to the spirit plane, is always there waiting for them to cross over, but many times they will choose to stay for awhile longer on the Earth plane. This is due to their emotions about their past physical life. Earth-bound spirits do not wish to let go of some part of their past physical life. Some human beings can see these Earth-bound spirits. This is because some human beings have their sixth sense activated.

Earth-bound spirit beings usually trust human beings. This is why a human being who can see and hear them will, at times, be able to lead them back into the light, back to the spirit plane. Earth-bound spirits are on a lower vibration, a lower frequency, because their soul is heavy with emotional pain. You know how you feel when your emotions are very unstable. You may feel bogged down—not light. These Earth-bound spirits feel troubled and wish to, at times, share their misery and torment with others. This is why there are hauntings of certain places and people. Understand beloved children of God, you must always put the white light of God around you, your family and your home, twice daily. This will protect you, your family, and home from any unwanted visits from these Earth-bound spirits who can carry misery with them.

Now, it is important to say there are some Earth-bound spirits that are not so negative. Their presence may even seem to be pleasant at times. Understand dear ones, all Earth-bound spirits are the lost souls of the universe. They are lost by their own accord. Because it is not healthy for a spirit being to stay Earth-bound, their energy may not always be compatible with your energy. This is why it is imperative that you ask God, the Father, to put His white light around you, your family, and your home and pets twice daily. This always insures your protection from any harmful, unwanted, or incompatible spirit energies. Also to pray twice a day greatly strengthens your connection with God, the Father. Your God-mind is open and activated with prayer to God.

PART 12:

SUICIDE

It is very unsettling for me (Saint Germain) to hear some of the false information given to people on the subject of suicide, because there is some confusion about what actually happens when a human being takes their own life. Beloved souls of God, every being, both human or spirit is loved and cherished by God, the Father in Heaven. God is love, pure love energy—the greatest love you can ever know and feel. God does not condemn any of His children to live eternity in Hell. It is complete nonsense for any person to write this or say this is true. Break down the word non-sense. It means no sense—no truth. God welcomes all of His children to join Him in an eternal life of love, joy, and peace. All they must do is ask God and it will be done. If any being, be it human or spirit, lives in Hell, it is by their own will—not God's.

Now when a person takes their own life, they will follow the same channels as other spirit beings who have just departed from their physical body. All people who have committed suicide are allowed to dwell in the light and love of God, if they so wish. Yes, it is a sin to kill, even oneself. And this sin will be addressed in the life review and Akashic Record discussion. You see, beloved children of God, when you set the plan in motion to come into another physical life incarnation on Earth, you have certain goals which you wish to attain while in that life. You discuss these goals and ambitions with God, the Father, and a record of them is made before you incarnate. What the person did not have an opportunity to accomplish due to the untimely death of the physical life will be discussed in the life review and Akashic Record discussion (past life record) and these goals will be carried over into another physical life incarnation.

Please understand this, beloved souls, God and every force of God's light, never wishes to see any person take their own life—ever. This is truth. All the love and assistance you or any person could ever want, need, or desire, awaits you. All you need to do is *ask*—pray to God. God hears every prayer and answers every prayer. All of God's children must have faith, for faith opens the door, so to speak, so that you will be able to see how God, the Father, is answering your prayers and guiding you. Without faith and hope you have "closed the door" to God's help. Your faith brings the loving help, guidance, and assistance from God and all who serve His will into your life and your loved one's lives. God is total perfection. You will find your strength and comfort through God and only God.

Many times people of Earth have heard or read that God, the Father, is an angry God. This is not truth! Anger is a negative emotion generated by fear. God is the opposite of fear. God, our Father is not negative in any way—ever. However, it is important to make clear there is an emotion and feeling called "righteous anger." God, the Father does feel righteous anger toward some of His children due to their actions. Righteous anger does not condemn anyone into Hell—ever. God does not hold righteous anger toward anyone who has committed suicide. Also understand, beloved souls, God is not pleased with the abuse human beings are responsible for on this planet. God, the Father, is disappointed in some of the actions of some of His children. God does not want abuse of any kind or form to be done to any of His Creation. God, the Father, wants the best for all of His children and Creation. This also stands true for the human beings who have committed suicide. God does not hold them in an abusive state after the human beings have taken their own lives. Understand, beloved ones, God forgives ALL. God loves ALL unconditionally—always.

So fear not, beloved people of the Earth, for your loved ones who have taken their life... committed suicide—*are NOT condemned by God and forced to live in damnation and Hell for any length of time.* They are not forced to be Earth-bound for any amount of years or time, as you may have read or been told. (Remember, spirit beings have no real concept of linear time.) If any spirit being lives in "hell" (in the lower astral plane) or is Earth-bound, it is by the spirit being's own will. They can come back to join God, the Father, at any time, if they wish. God opens His arms to all His children. God, the Father, and all His forces of light, all His angels, all the Ascended Masters, welcome ALL who wish to be with God, our Father, and live in His love and light. This forever holds true for any human being who lives on Earth and any spirit being who has died the physical death and wishes to cross over into the Light. I hope I have put your hearts and minds at rest and at peace with this information.

PART 13:

HOLDING ON TO THE SORROW

At this time, I Saint Germain, wish to reflect on what takes place when the people of Earth feel much sadness and great sorrow when their loved ones have departed from their physical life. Again, there is some confusion concerning this subject. It is my intention to "clear the air," so to speak.

As you know, when a person leaves their physical life to return to spirit life, the people who loved this person who "died" will, of course, mourn—feel very sad, and many times feel great emotional and mental and even physical pain. This is a normal—painful, but normal—process for a human being to experience. It is the process of grieving. This process usually takes much time to heal. Some people may never "heal" from this loss in their lives. Always know, beloved souls, know in your heart and mind, these people who have "died" are *not dead*. Spirits are not dead. If they *were* dead, I, Saint Germain, would not be coming through and speaking to this oracle as she is writing my words. *NO ONE DIES!* Spirit beings are energy, an energy that is part of and one with God, our Father. Spirit energy is infinite. God's energy is eternal—everlasting. Human beings are energy also. However, this energy is the outer casing of your spirit's eternal energy. Human beings' energy is limited to only the third dimension. Spirit being energy is inter-dimensional.

Now, it has been written and said by some people that when people feel such pain and sorrow that they cannot let go of their loved one, that this actually keeps the spirit from moving on within the spirit plane. This is not 100% true for all spirit beings. It is true that thoughts are energy, and emotions are energy. This sorrowful energy from the people of Earth, if it is strong enough, can somewhat affect the spirit being it is directed to. This does not necessarily mean they are stuck and cannot graduate into the Light of the spirit world (spirit plane).

Understand, beloved souls, there is always love and healing given by God, the Father, to all His Creation, and these spirit beings who feel this sorrow from the Earth plane, many times can and do send you healing comfort and love from God. This sending of love and healing from God to Earth will become another part of the spirit being's work in the spirit plane or spirit world (as some wish to refer to it). However, it is important to make clear, some spirit beings will have a more difficult time feeling at peace or feeling comfortable, when they feel a wave of this sad and distressing energy from their loved ones on Earth. At this time, if the spirit being wishes, much assistance is offered by the spirit's guides, angels, any Ascended Masters, and always by God, the Father, to help both the person or persons on Earth as well as the spirit being to be comforted and helped through these emotional and painful times.

A spirit being always has their own will. No thing can ever change that. However, some spirit beings do feel emotionally harmed when there is strong sorrow felt by loved ones from the Earth plane. This will sometimes inhibit their moving on. This is only because they have not accepted the love assistance from God that has been offered to them by all the loving beings who serve God in spirit. Then on the other side of this (pardon the pun), there are some spirit beings who take the sorrow and pain that is felt from people who love them, and turn this suffering into love and healing. Love releases pain. For example, Princess

Diana is doing quite well in the spirit plane. She had a period of adjustment where she and God, the Father, sent love and healing energy to all the people of Earth who mourned her death. She is a beacon of light in the spirit world, where she is loved and adored by all.

So you see beloved souls, it is very possible for spirit beings to give love and healing to the people of Earth and it is always possible for the spirit being to receive healing and love from God when there is great emotional sorrow. Always know, beloved ones, you can receive healing and love from God at any time and at all times. You do not have to endure pain and suffering for the loss of a loved one. You are *never* alone, no matter how "alone" or desolate you may feel. In every reality you are not alone—*ever!* God's great love will surround you and comfort you. All you need to do is ask God and you will know God's love, comfort, and assistance is with you, for you will feel it. Pray to God anywhere, anytime. God our Loving Father, is always with you. All you need is strong faith, for your faith is the foundation to your connection to God. When you are connected to God, you will feel His love take hold of your grief and sorrow, and replace it with comfort, strength and the knowing that your loved ones are very much alive. When you are strongly connected to God, you will be able to feel your angel give you love, and help you through the hard times. God and all His angels and all God's Forces of Light understand your pain and are always willing and very happy to give assistance in the name of the Holy Father, God, to all His children who cry out for help.

At times of great sorrow, it is important for the people of Earth to give great effort to release anger and fear, no matter how tragic the cause of death of your loved one. You must understand, beloved souls, every Earth life has a plan. You do not know the details of everyone's Earth life plan. This is a sacred contract every spirit being discusses with God. Before the spirit being incarnates into an Earth life, the spirit being will make a contract and plan out what their life will be like on Earth. Many of you do not know the details of your *own* Earth life plan. So you see, beloved souls, it is not likely you will know the Earth life plan of those people close to you. This is why the Lord Jesus said, "Judge not." The main reason for this is because you do not always know what is Divine Order.

Some people may choose a tragic death to rectify their karma, or maybe for some other purpose that serves Divine Order. God's universe is always under Divine Order. God forgives all and God heals all—always. God loves you. God loves all His children eternally. So understand, beloved souls, God and all His Forces of Light can see your pain. We know of the emotional distress you feel. If you turn to God at every difficult moment, you will, without fail, be given love, strength, and comfort. All you ever need is your faith.

As people's feelings of great sorrow can, at times, affect the spirit beings by making them sad and uncomfortable, the opposite of this is also true. If people would turn their feelings of sadness and despair into loving prayers and good thoughts for their loved ones who have "died," then these spirit beings would be able to adjust and heal (if necessary) more quickly and with great joy because you have sent them love energy. You may think this is impossible. Understand and know always, beloved souls, (as the saying goes), "All things are possible with God."

Nothing is impossible when you have God, the Father's love and assistance with you. All beings, human and spirit, who serve God await to serve *you.* All you must do is ask and have faith.

With my love to you always,

Saint Germain,
received by Eve Barbieri

✠ Chapter 15 ✠

AFFIRMATIONS

by
Saint Germain

✥ AFFIRMATIONS ✥

Hello and many greetings of love. This is Saint Germain. Tonight I wish to give you some brief knowledge on your thoughts and also offer to you some all-powerful **I AM** affirmations. First I will reflect on how your thoughts create for you. As we all have said many times in this book, your thoughts are power, and they create for you. Thoughts are *energy* and energy creates, both the positive and negative. Understand, beloved souls, your entire life and your entire destiny is determined by your thoughts. Your thoughts—every thought you have—paves your life path. As an example, if you *think* you are unattractive or *not good enough* for someone to love you, then your thoughts will bring to you people who will also *think* you are not good enough to love. If you *think* you are not worthy of having money, then those thoughts of low self-worth will bring to your life a lack of all worth. You see, beloved souls, your thoughts are energy and energy vibrates and this is a subtle, but powerful, form of communication to others.

Human beings are extremely perceptive and are influenced by these vibrations. That is why when you go to a place where a person is very angry, you can feel the tense energy in the air. You are actually affected by this energy, whether it is good energy or negative energy. The same is true when you visit a place that is peaceful; your body and mind will feel more at ease. This energy vibration communicates with all the embodiments of human beings. So if there are thoughts of low self-esteem, people will *pick up* on that vibration and their thoughts and opinions will be influenced by that energy. If you think and truly know in your heart you are worthy of all good and all of

God's glorious blessings, then your life will be filled with blessings and goodness. You will, without fail, bring this goodness to yourself and to your life. Your thoughts of self-worth will create an energy vibration of self-empowerment. This self-empowerment energy vibration will radiate all around you, uplifting you out of a self-defeating attitude. This powerful vibration of light energy will empower all that you are. Your physical, mental, emotional, and spiritual embodiments will begin to be healed when you commence this empowering transformation. Even your physical body's immune system will be enhanced with every positive thought, with every powerful, positive affirmation, and with every prayer to God, the Father. This great, powerful energy vibration not only uplifts and empowers your being and your soul, but also helps to uplift and empower all other people you come into contact with. This is what some people call "the good vibrations."

You are a wonderful, glorious, human being, who is truly, unconditionally, and forever loved by God, the Father. You have greatness within you. Divine greatness is forever held within all of God's glorious Creation. The third-dimensional world is one of great illusion. Your society today is one that passes much judgment onto all. I, Saint Germain, ask you people of Earth to see into the illusion and see past the judgment and to self-empower and uplift yourself with positive thoughts, prayers, and affirmations. By doing so, you will stop forever the downward spiral that has affected some of the lives of the people on Earth. Instead, you can create for yourself and your families a life that is fulfilled with all the blessings of God.

We who serve the Father, God, in the spiritual realms understand that humans on Earth may *think* this achievement of self-empowerment through positive thought is a difficult task.

This, beloved souls, is total illusion. It is true, there has been much negative programming of the human mind throughout the eons of time. However, to change your personal mindset is indeed much easier than you may think. All one must do is to stay focused and determined, to always keep their faith in God strong, and most of all—be positive. This thought transformation into self-empowerment and a positive lifestyle that is filled with love and blessings from God, our Father, can be obtained. This choice is yours. You may stay locked into illusion, into a world of fear and judgment. Or you may choose to be liberated, free from the outer experiences, and to go within yourself to be an empowered being, a human being of love and light. To begin this mighty and glorious transformation, you must begin each day with positive affirmations and also prayers to God, the Father. An affirmation is a powerful suggestive statement that changes the human mindset. I will now give you some examples of self-empowering **I AM** affirmations.

I AM one with God, the creator of this world and all worlds.

I AM loved unconditionally and for all eternity by God, my creator.

I AM in love with myself.

I AM worthy of all the love in this universe.

I AM worthy of all the goodness that exists to come into my life.

I AM living this day and each day of my life in perfect and optimum health.

I AM a powerful being of love, and I choose my own destiny.

I AM receiving guidance, love, and protection from God at all times.

I AM free of all diseases, illnesses, and sickness, this day and all the days of my life.

I AM free of all pain, always.

I AM free of all fear, anger, and hatred this day and all the days of my life.

I AM patient, kind, and gentle to myself and my fellow man.

I AM living in harmony with all of God's glorious Creation.

I AM in fellowship with God, his angels, and his elite Forces of Light.

I AM peaceful.

These are good examples of some very powerful, positive, I AM affirmations. If you wish, you may say these every day to yourself and to God. Or if you wish, you can always think and create positive and powerful affirmations that you can tailor to the specific issues and circumstances in your life. However, if I may, I wish to offer some advice. When you are giving thought to your specific affirmations, it is best to use positive language terms, and speak in the present tense, and not in the future. It is advised, when you affirm, that you rid yourself of the term, "I will," because the term, "I will" exists in the future and does not apply to present time. Your affirmations should be what you desire for today, for to say what you desire "already exists" creates it **now**. Also, it is better to say, "I am free of pain," rather than to say "I am not feeling pain." This is because the word "not" has a less freeing ability and there is a more negative overtone associated with that particular word. To say "I am free of…" is truly more liberating. It is much better to tell yourself you are free of something negative, rather than to tell yourself you are not going to have it. To free yourself and to liberate yourself is to uplift yourself. And to uplift yourself will raise you up and out of the mindset of illusion and falsehoods. Always remember, beloved souls, you are powerful beings, with the absolute power to create your own destiny through your thoughts and your prayers to God. With positive thoughts and diligent prayer to God, our Father, and strong, lasting faith, you can surely change your life for the better and pave a very bright path for your future. If you ever feel alone, and/or you need support, please know that God is always there for you. Call on Him. Call on any of the Ascended Masters, including myself, Saint Germain, or the angels of God, or the archangels, if you wish. All of us that I have mentioned serve the Lord God and are willing and eager to help and give assistance to any and all of humanity at any time. Beloved souls, I ask that you deep breathe often, drink plenty of water, give much thought to all your thoughts, and go in peace. God and all the heavens love you. My love is with you always.

Saint Germain,
received by Eve Barbieri

CHAPTER 16

DIVINE DECREES

by
The Lord Jesus Christ

✤ DIVINE DECREES ✤

Greetings and love to all. This is Jesus of Nazareth and I have come to give you some information on creating with decrees. Decrees are similar to affirmations. The main difference is the authority with which the statements are made. When a king issues a decree, it becomes a law. Such is the authority and power of a decree.

Affirmations are a way of reprogramming your mind to think in a certain way. They tell your subconscious mind what you want, which attracts the energy required to bring it to you. Correct thinking is the first step to Self-mastery and taking control of your life.

When you issue a decree, however, you put forth a command into the ethers and it is done according to your words. Great care must be exercised when making decrees. They should be made with only the purest and holiest of intent and for the highest good of all—for the power of your intent is indeed great. To make a decree without much prayer and thought is to create chaos.

A decree can be a most powerful tool for good. When you issue a decree, a great wave of energy is created to accomplish your words. If everyone decreed peace, or the Kingdom of God on Earth, the mindset of man would change drastically through the energies of this decree within the ethers.

Great care must be taken when issuing decrees for yourself or another. Choose your words carefully and with much thought and prayer. Remember, you are creating a law and putting it into effect. Take care that you do not try to manipulate the life of another by decreeing for them that which would not be in their best interests. This would cause some degree of havoc in their lives, even if you meant well. Let me give you an example.

Suppose a loved one is seriously ill and you wish to help by issuing a decree. To issue a decree for *health* may not serve them, in that they are completing a life lesson through their illness. Now, to issue a decree for *healing* is good, in that it helps them to heal that which is out of balance in their whole being, including their soul. This may result in their physical healing also, or it may not, depending on their life plan. If they are not healed physically, they can be helped to adjust better and learn their lessons quicker and easier. They can be happier and have more joy within their present circumstances. This is how to help another with your decrees. It must always be for your and another's *highest good.*

Your words have great power. That is why it is written, "By your words you will be justified, and by your words you will be condemned (or judged)." In a decree, your words are sent forth with authority. You must *believe* in your heart that you deserve whatever good you wish to decree for yourself. If you decree a new car, but in your heart you doubt you will get one, it will be much more difficult to bring it to pass. This is why it is often easier to decree for another, as this element of self-worth is not an issue. When a king or queen issues a decree or makes a law, they have no doubt that it will be honored.

There is also strength in numbers, in that—say there is a group of people and one of them is having a problem. The group can then decree a peaceful and fair solution to the problem for them, which would be most helpful. Families can decree a peaceful and loving atmosphere in their home. The more this is done, the more powerful it becomes, for each time the decree is issued, new waves of energy are created, amplifying those from the previous decrees.

When you make a decree, do so with great care, and then issue your decrees with the authority of a son or daughter of the Most High God, and it will be done. It is also suggested that you keep a record of your decrees, for obvious reasons.

This is a power given to you by Divine Authority. If you were a king or queen of a nation, you would not make laws haphazardly, but would consider well before doing so. This is how you are to approach your decrees. When the situation calls for it, use this tool with a pure heart and the purest of motives, and all will be well. When you worry, you give more energy to the problem. When you issue a decree, you can turn that energy around toward the solution. I AM always here to guide you whenever you need me. My blessings are upon each of you.

The Lord Jesus Christ,
received by Romayne de Kanter

Chapter 17

TELEPATHY

by
The Holy Spirit/The Great White Brotherhood of God

✦ TELEPATHY ✦

We, the Brotherhood of God, known as the Holy Spirit, greet you in the love of the Father. Today, we wish to give you an understanding of telepathy and how it works.

Telepathy is the ability to communicate mind to mind with another being. This could be a person or an animal. All animals have consciousness, so this is possible, and it transcends the language barrier.

The ability for mind-to-mind communication is present within all beings. The rational mind has come to regard this form of communication as unrealistic and unnatural. If it cannot be recognized through the five senses, then it is not considered valid. So you have created various devices that are used for the purpose of contacting one another.

We would suggest however, that you begin in some small way to mentally—through the realm of thought—endeavor to communicate with another. Often, human beings have a difficult time saying certain things to each other. When face to face, they become self-conscious or embarrassed, and words are hard to find. Letters are sometimes used in these circumstances. But few realize that all can be said in the mind.

We would suggest that you begin to develop this gift from God by sending thoughts of love to those dear to you. Whether they are in the same room, or thousands of miles away, the effect is the same. You can do this in many ways. There is no wrong way to do this, and each person will develop their own method. You will know it is working by the results you get. For those who wish to try this, we will offer a few ideas for you to work with. Start by saying their name and picture them in your mind. This is sort of like calling them on the telephone and it gets their attention mentally so that they are then "tuned into you." Imagine yourself greeting them and speaking with them as though they were right there with you. Listen with your heart. This is also a good way to heal any troubles or misunderstandings, for each can be honest in this neutral space. With a little practice, you will discover how easy it is to send your messages this way. Relationships will be enhanced and life will be more peaceful for all.

This is a good way to ask your boss for a raise without being nervous or stressed, or the fear of being turned down. We are sure that if you use your imagination, you can find many instances where this technique would be quite useful. You can talk to your children while they sleep during the night and they will not turn a deaf ear to you, as they sometimes do when they are awake.

Now this is not to say that you can use this gift to manipulate another in any way or to do harm. If you attempt to do this, you place yourself in harm's way first and foremost. I assure you, dear ones, you will not like the results Always use this gift with love and purity of heart, and you will be blessed.

Have fun with this new tool of learning. If you are in need of guidance, we are ever at your service.

The Great White Brotherhood of God,
received by Romayne de Kanter

✛ CHAPTER 18 ✛

TRANSFORMATION

by
Saint Germain

✛ TRANSFORMATION ✛

Greetings to all from St. Germain of the Kingdom of Light. Today we will discuss transformation and the role of the violet flame, which is my gift to the world.

This powerful flame is a manifestation of the violet ray, the ray on which the new age of peace enters your world. The words "Thy kingdom come" are literal, for indeed that is the process. The Kingdom of God is truly upon this ray. When it reaches your world, the Kingdom will be established there.

As the ray comes nearer, you will begin to feel its effects. It is the master cleanser. It brings all that it touches into a state of extreme purity. This can result in some degree of upheaval in your world for there is much that needs cleaning up. This can seem traumatic and can result in much suffering. Yet it is necessary. As gold is purified by fire, so are all things purified by "fires" of various kinds. Even your very souls are purified by the "fiery trials" in your life. So when you see these things come to pass, know that it is both good and necessary, and do not despair. To be pure is to be in the One—the state of wholeness and Oneness with God. All of Creation yearns to be in this perfect state. The planet must be prepared for the Kingdom of God. Dis-ease is rampant on the planet at this time and nothing—NO THING—is pure, not the air, not the water, not the land—NO THING. This is not allowed and will be corrected, for God has heard the cries of anguish from His Creation. God does not care about your fine buildings. These are the creations of man as temples to himself.

The corrections that occur are systematic, not occurring at random. This purification process has been designed to take place in a most effective and orderly manner. This reverses the entire process of dis-ease. Much thought, planning and preparation have gone into this process. As I direct my flame of purification through the various phases, great changes will occur.

Ask for my flame to purify your hearts, your souls and all that is you. It can work with you gently now, as you give it permission. This is a much gentler purification process than the latter one, where you will be "*thrown* into the fire," so to speak. ALL MUST BE PURE—NO EXCEPTIONS. All WILL be pure by Divine Decree—and so it is.

Thank you for your service.

Saint Germain,
received by Romayne de Kanter

CHAPTER 19

COLOR AND DISEASE

by
The Lord Jesus Christ

✤ COLOR AND DISEASE ✤

Greetings to all. This is Jesus, bringing you loving messages from the Holy Realms. Today we will discuss some causes of disease.

All disease starts from within. You think it is caused by "germs," but that is only an illusion. The breakdown of the body begins at the auric level and progresses toward the physical. Healing also begins in this way. Maintaining a strong aura is the key to eliminating disease from the human condition.

How do you keep your aura strong? The ways are many. Meditation is one way. Meditating with color—the rays in particular—bring many aspects of the vibratory spectrum into the human energy field. This is a complicated system. Allow me to give a brief overview.

Within your aura or energy field, there is what is known as your etheric body. This energy body is an exact duplicate of your physical body, with all its organs and limbs, etc. As the color flows into the subconscious mind during color meditations, the vibrations of the colors adjust the various organs in the etheric body and the process of healing begins. The healing vibrations are then filtered into the physical body by impulses, giving proper nourishment to these organs and normal function is restored. This may be immediate, or it may take some time relative to the damage within the organ. One day man will begin to use color in this way. Color chambers will be constructed and medicine as it is now will be a thing of the past.

The rainbow and its colors are the key. All the colors of the rainbow exist in your energy field, as well as some colors that are not known in your world. Disease is the result of a lack of one or more of these rainbow colors in sufficient quantity and quality to maintain health.

With practice, you can learn to stand apart from your body and check out the quality of color in your energy field. This is done with the mind in a meditative state. You can then add more color where it is needed while you are in this meditative state. You can also do it physically with food. The colors of your foods give you a clue. They have been given colors to assist you in keeping the body functioning properly. For example, greens help the heart center or chakra. Oranges and lemons help the stomach. Red beets help the root chakra and strengthen the blood. So if you are out of balance, eat more of the foods of the color you need. It is important to bless the food before you eat it. Today it is filled with much in the way of chemical compounds that are not good for the body. Prayer renders these chemicals harmless and increases nutrient value, as it restores life back into the food.

Now understand, dear children of the Father, it is the bright-ness and hue of the rainbow colors that produce health. When you look at the rainbow, the colors are rich and clear, bright and beautiful. These are the hues you want.

There are also colors or hues that produce illness. For instance, you have a term, "green with envy." This shade of green is not found in the rainbow. It is a shade of green that is muddied, a sickly green. Someone who is ill often has a certain "green" cast to them when they are pale.

Another example is a dark, blood red, which is not pleasant to look at. You would not want to paint your room this color or that sickly green, as it would be very disturbing to your energy field. Your thoughts and emotions also produce colors in your aura. Thoughts of love are associated with bright red and pinks. When you are feeling "blue," there is a shade of blue-gray within your aura. When you feel hopeless, it is a dark grey or black. When you are happy, it is a sunny yellow or orange.

As you have probably guessed, the process also works in reverse. More yellow around you will lift your spirits. More pink will draw more love. More red will energize. More green will balance, and more blue will calm and is good for anxiety.

Experiment with color and how it can enrich your life and heal your body. This is a free gift from your Loving Father that has been forgotten. All beings love a rainbow and are blessed by the rays of light emanating from it. It is God's promise of eternal love.

As you work with the rainbow, you will come to appreciate color and its effects. Flowers bring color, aroma, and have an essence that lifts the spirit in a most special way. Make them a part of your life, for they are healing for your emotions and bring much beauty into your life. As you can see, your Heavenly Father has thought of everything for your joy and well-being. You have only to discover these wonders that you take for granted.

I, Lord Jesus, bless you in your travels through the rainbow.

The Lord Jesus Christ,
received by Romayne de Kanter

✤ CHAPTER 20 ✤

THE CRYSTAL

by
Archangel Michael

✤ THE CRYSTAL ✤

Greetings, beloved ones. This is the Archangel Michael. The purpose for this writing is to bring to you some knowledge about the crystal. The tapping into the knowledge of the crystal has changed life as you know it on the planet Earth. You have vastly broadened the horizon of technology in your everyday lives to the point to where you have become dependent on this advanced knowledge.

The crystal has in it a new world of knowing. It contains silicon. Silicon is made up of small, tiny, prisms of light—thousands and thousands of them. These prisms are endless in the information they hold. Understand, beloved souls, light is information. Light is given to you from God, the Father in Heaven. These prisms have been broken down into very small chips, the kind found in computers. The people who have pioneered this technology, who have brought it into an understanding, have had much help and guidance from the Masters in the universe. This guidance was needed for mankind to advance this far in your evolution.

However, there have been some setbacks in the pace of your advancement. The technologists have refused to hear some very important guidance given to them for the purposes of safety and balance on the planet. Because of this, there are certain situations where God, the Father, has needed to intervene. Understand, this knowledge is universal knowledge. The incorporating of this technology has put people into a new cycle, a new day and age to work with. However, this new age of technology has come with its own set of problems for the planet Earth. The pollution this new advancement in technology

has caused your planet is astronomical. There are heavy pollutants in your water supply, your air supply, and in the ground.
Because of this, the planet Earth is off-balance.

Understand, the crystals are the true energy sources in the
Mother Earth. These are her true gemstones. Because of these
fabulous little tools given to you, the people of this planet, by
God, the Father, and Mother Earth, your advancement has
been changed for as long as the Earth will stay in this state.
These numerous prisms of light have the power to bring to
mind facts you have never imagined. The energy in one crystal
is infinite. It knows no limits. What man has done is unlock
the code—decoded the prisms of light into a new science, the
science of the crystal. It is also known as "utilization of silicon."
This using of silicon is the first stage of finding the higher
knowledge of the universe. The crystal has inside of it many
different aspects. There are aspects of the crystal that can lead
you in to see and hear other worlds—other planets—to
communicate with the other beings who dwell on these other
planets. These systems contained in the many different aspects
of these crystals have not been decoded. They have not been
figured out at this present time. Whether or not these systems
of advanced, infinite knowledge will ever be decoded and
utilized on planet Earth by the people who are the technologists of this planet will depend on the collective consciousness
of mankind.

Understand, beloved souls, these very highly developed and
intricate systems can only be decoded, be put into knowledge
in the minds of man, if mankind has made total peace with
itself. When the level of consciousness is raised, so is the
absolute intelligence of man. This process of finding total love

and peace for all of God, the Father's Creation is what is needed for man's mind to evolve enough to have the ability to unlock this knowledge and understand this knowledge, and put it into this world. These higher aspects of knowledge found in the crystals are to be unlocked and decoded when—and only when—the minds and hearts of man know, live by, and hold dear to them peace, love, compassion, kindness, and non-judgment. The God-mind must join and become one with the mind of man before any of these highly advanced technologies will ever be given to the people of Earth. This is for your safety and the safety of those in other worlds.

There are some fun things you can do with the crystals to bring their powerful, wonderful love energy into your aura and into your being. You can program them, the crystals, into your energy. You can, if you wish, start by holding the crystal in your left hand and focus love energy from your third eye into the crystal. This starts the process of activating the energies of the love vibration of the crystal into your being. Hold the crystal during your meditation, during your prayers, when you are not feeling well, and when you are angry and upset. By doing so—holding the crystal during prayer and meditation—the crystal will heighten your awareness during these sacred times. By holding them during times of distress, illness, anger, and upheavals, the crystal will bring healing and balance to the situation and to your body.

The crystal holds much wondrous power and love from the Heavenly Father and Mother Earth. These crystals are one of the many gifts of love from God, our Father in the Heavens. These precious gemstones of the planet can and do offer to you much love and healing for use in your everyday lives. These precious crystals are to be cherished and respected at all times by you. Understand, beloved souls, the great infinite power of love from God, the Father, is in the ground of Mother Earth, and can be in your hands and into your being. Be in peace. With love—

Archangel Michael,
received by Eve Barbieri

CHAPTER 21

CHANGE

by
The Lord Jesus Christ

✣ CHANGE ✣

Peace and love from the realms of Light. This is Jesus and I have come to speak to you about change. Are you all settled in your world? Is your life one of predictability? How do you view change? Is it stressful, or joyous? When I came to Earth, I upset the status quo. I changed people's lives in a big way—for the better, to be sure, but change nonetheless.

The more you resist change, the harder you make it for yourself. To "go with the flow" means to be flexible and adjust to whatever changes come to you with grace and faith. It makes no sense to get upset. You must bend like a tree in the wind, yielding, dancing with the breeze.

Changes must come. Great ones and small ones. They are part of life and its experiences. They make life interesting.

It is fear that makes you resist—fear of the unknown and where the change will take you. Fear keeps you trapped in your comfort zone—afraid to branch out and be all you can be— use all of your God-given talents, or even discover what they are. You will not make a mistake if you follow your dreams. There are no wrong changes as you follow your inner guidance. Your desires are calling to you for a reason. As you step out in faith you will find that which you seek. All change is good. It is a teacher. Make it your friend.

My love and support is always there for you to draw upon. Go in peace.

The Lord Jesus Christ,
received by Romayne de Kanter

CHAPTER 22

ANGER

by
The Holy Spirit/The Great White Brotherhood of God

✤ ANGER ✤

We, the Holy Spirit, wish to speak a little to you about anger. Anger is a demonic force. By demonic, we say it is produced by fear. The dark forces feed on people's fear. When you look at the positive side to any situation, then you have taken control over that situation, thereby conquering fear. Understand, your life has many emotional sides to it. You have your funny, happy, joyful, faithful, confident (self-confident) emotions. Then you have—if you give it power, **your** power—the negative side to this, which is fear, anger, hatred, control, and ego. Fear is the main source of all these negative emotions. Your fear grants power to any dark beings who may be nearby, waiting to see how they can take and destroy. They are like the vultures of the astral plane. Now the vultures (the birds that God created) clean up the land to beautify it and make it pure. The dark beings litter and pollute wherever they go. They can gently talk to the subconscious mind of people to influence their thoughts and actions. All they need is a little fear and ego in that person and they (the dark beings) are off and running, so to speak.

This is one of the reasons we ask you to stay away from television. Watching television shows will program the subconscious mind to lie dormant, resulting in a subconscious block of energy flow. This allows the mind to play an inactive role in thought forms and thought patterns. It takes away your power of discernment—the knowing of what is right or what is wrong for you individually. It is at that point that the dark beings can easily come through into someone's mind. The subconscious is what allows you to go within and connect, be one with God. Your subconscious is your God-mind. When that energy is stopped (blocked), fear steps in and the dark beings have the power they need to do their destructive will. Breathe, beloved souls. Breathe deeply and for a lengthy period of time. This allows for the subconscious energy to flow again and expands your aura to make it strong. When you are tired, breathe. When you are happy, breathe. When you are sad, breathe. When you are angry, breathe. Breathe often. This allows the anger to subside, to be dissolved—to be of no harm to you or anyone else.

We are not trying to preach to you about meditation. However, to sit and breathe deeply for about three minutes puts you, your mind, your body and spirit in a meditative state, the state of Alpha-consciousness. You do not have to try to imagine a safe place or a particular place. If you can and you do, then even better. However, it is not necessary. All that is always necessary is to breathe deeply and continuously, and drink adequate amounts of water. That is all that is necessary to connect your mind with your spirit self. Your spirit self is what channels light into your physical body to cure diseases and illnesses and addictions. There are many other tools which will speed this process along, such as prayer (diligent prayer to God, the Father in Heaven), positive affirmations, faith, and to love yourself and appreciate who you are, what you are to the world and to God. You are God's precious child. Love yourself as God loves you. And also to give love and respect to all of God's Creation. Respect and love your enemies. Know that this is where they are on their own spiritual path in relationship to God. Free your heart of judgments. We know this can be challenging at times. Understand it is a challenge easily conquered when there is love in your heart, love for all of God's Creation—from every tree and bush to every animal, dog and cat, and to every person— no matter who they are or what they have done. You are not the ones assigned to pass and give judgment. That job is only for God, the Father, Creator of this and all universes. We give you all of our love from God. Always walk in peace.

The Great White Brotherhood of God,
received by Eve Barbieri

CHAPTER 23

GREED

by
The Lord Jesus Christ

✤ GREED ✤

Greetings and all my love to the world. This is the Lord Jesus Christ. My thought today is to bring to you some information on the subject of *Greed*. Greed is a very harmful mindset. It is selfish in all respects. Greed breeds contempt of the power of Divine Love. A person who is greedy has very little room in their heart for love and the joy of the gift of giving. They have only their own wants in mind—how they can be more pleased in their own lives. Understand—greed is a vicious cycle. Through greed, a massive circle of fear is born. One thinks they do not have enough. They are in fear of never having enough. Therefore they will continue to take and keep only for themselves. This leaves little room for faith and allowing themselves to trust in God, the Father to provide what is needed. No man can ever provide for you all you need in this life or any life. God is the only Source to obtain all that you need. Money cannot possibly fulfill every desire. This is illusion. Money can only buy you luxuries—pleasures of the flesh, not pleasures of the heart. The people who are so involved with the pleasures of the flesh have a void in their heart. This void leads them into fear and temptation, thinking they had better get all they can for themselves. The emotion of the heart is empty. Their heart, and the feeling of satisfaction is not fulfilled.

You say, "How can this be? They look so happy and have so much—so many beautiful things." Understand, beloved ones, children of God, the Father in the Heavens, an *object*—no matter how beautiful or how expensive—can never bring to you total happiness. This is only temporary. The emotion of giving is the only way to fill the heart. An inanimate object, no matter what this may be, can only bring a shallow feeling of happiness. There is no true substance to this emotion. I am not saying to you to give up everything you own or that you cannot have nice things in your home, or a car to drive. What I am saying is that when you focus only on what you have and how you can have more—be it money or material items—then you have truly lost your connection to Spirit, to our Father, God in Heaven.

You are not more special to God if you have more money than the next man. Money is of no importance to God, other than how people use it to help and give to others—to the other children of this, His world. Money is a man-made energy, used as a means of exchange on your planet. The only time it becomes part of spiritual energy is when it is used to help the less fortunate, the ones who have less in this world. Your feelings, your life here on Earth is, by all means of knowing, more valued by God and His forces of Light than any dollar amount. I, Lord Jesus am quoted in the Bible as saying, "It would be easier for a camel to go through the eye of a needle than for a rich man to enter the Kingdom of Heaven." This is truth. Understand—the riches and luxuries of the wealthy are only an illusion. The true riches and wealth, beyond what you could ever know in your mind and heart, lie in the Kingdom of God in this universe and all universes. Beautiful, large homes and expensive cars offer no emotional fulfillment. They are empty. They leave the person in a state of lack. This is the dark side tricking you to keep you away from the real importance of life, which is to be one with God, the Father, King of the Universe.

Many people are so preoccupied in their minds and in the actions of life to make more and more money that they have forgotten where they have come from. All of you people, every one who breathes on the planet Earth, was created by God and only God. Your mother birthed you into this world, giving you breath. It is God, the Father, our King of the Light in all worlds, who gave you life. To know this, to truly understand this and feel this in your heart, to be one with the Father God in Heaven, is the greatest gift, the greatest treasure and the most abundant wealth ever known and given to mankind.

People have the concept embedded in their minds that money can bring them the greatest treasures, the most happiness. This is false "truth." The *real truth* is to be free of the fear of not having enough. That is the greatest happiness. You may ask, "How can this be achieved?" I will answer by saying, "By putting your faith and trust in God, the Father. By praying to Him that you and your family will be provided for, that He— God, our Father—will give His blessing of love and protection to you and your family." You must understand, it is only through prayer, by the asking for God, the Father, to intervene and give you and your family His blessings, that God will do so. God does not impose Himself upon His children. However, He will always answer and grant your prayers.

That is not to say you are to ask God, our Father, for a million dollars. God will provide for you and your family, your needs and some of the wants—but not to be so very rich in money that you would lose your connection with Him. You see, money is a deterrent from God. Money, in large sums, will create distance from you and your true Creator. God will give to you His wealth, spiritual wealth. This creates for you a life of peace and Divine Love. Many of you do not know for one full day of linear time what it feels like to have true peace of mind. Everyone's mind is in a state of worry at some time, and for some, this state lasts for days. Understand, beloved ones created by God, when you are blessed with God's spiritual wealth, then at this time you will experience and know true peace of mind, and freedom from fear of the future, for your future is in the hands of God. In this place—the hands of God, King of this universe and all universes—is where total and complete security lies. Safety, confidence, love, and stability have their domain in the hands of God.

These qualities of life do not dwell in their true state in the hands of man. Understand, mankind cannot be totally trusted. God is to be totally and completely, 100% trusted. Deep in the hearts and minds of man lies fear. God is the opposite of fear. Fear leads mankind away from God to try to do for themselves. In this process, man is left to do for himself first. This creates an imbalance in the harmony of mankind. Understand this: Free will is invoked and present in the thoughts and actions of man every minute and every hour of every day on planet Earth. This free will gives people the choice to do what is good or what is evil. If you put your trust in a man who does evil, or a system that a man who does evil created, then you have given yourself and all you have to the evil. You have given yourself and all you have to a situation where you are at the disadvantage. God is the advantage. God, our Father is pure love. No evil would ever or could ever be presented into your life when you put your trust and faith in God. True blessings come from the inside out—not from the outer to you, not from the outer expressions of the world. True wealth is found in the Kingdom of Heaven, which is found within you—within your mind, your thoughts, your heart, your actions. This is true reality. In your heart is where your true reality lies, not in the outer world. No objects, no matter how beautiful, can bring to your heart true fulfillment.

True and absolute beauty is felt and known only by the love you give to yourself, to others, and to all of God's blessed Creation. You, children of God, please know and bring into your realization: Life, the breath of life, the breath of all life and Creation, is absolute beauty. Love is in your breath. God's almighty, cherished love is in all of Creation. Breathe. When your focus is on how much money and how many belongings you can have, then my dear ones, children of God, the Father, you have lost the feeling of love in your breath, the feeling of love in your soul. When you—all of you—die and leave this lifetime behind and return to the heavens to be with God in spirit, you will not bring anything of this world with you—not one *thing*. You will, without question, bring as an offering to God all of your good deeds and your charities. *This is the only reality that exists in this universe!* The money you have saved and hoarded, the beautiful homes and beautiful cars and expensive clothing will not be and never have been your reality. The gifts of love, of caring, compassion, kindness, and non-judgment are the beautiful, tangible gifts to God and to the others you have given these precious gifts to.

I, Lord Jesus, giver of peace and love to this world, request that you focus your attention on the gift of Love and caring to others in place of caring about making more and more money for yourself. The blessings which come from the change in your actions, the change of your focus, will be immeasurable in their abundance. Have the courage to *let go* of the mindset that is so prevalent in your society. Put your trust in God. Put all your faith in God. You—all of you—are God's children. Our Father God will never abandon His children. You must always ASK and keep on asking. Keep your connection with God open.

ASK for guidance and strength; it will be given to you. We are here to help and give to you all that is needed. It is only your own mind and thoughts that separate you from God, the Father, King of all Light in this universe and all universes. My love is always with you.

The Lord Jesus Christ,
received by Eve Barbieri

CHAPTER 24

PREJUDICE

by
***The Lord Jesus Christ
and Mother Mary***

✣ PREJUDICE ✣

Greetings and blessings to all who read these words with an open heart. The Father in Heaven has sent me to give you a message on a subject that is dear to Him. This is Jesus, and I have come to speak to you about race, color, and nationality.

You have heard the term, "Variety is the spice of life." This is a truth, for if everything were one color, one flower, one food, how very dull your life would be! Variety is found in every aspect of life, is it not? And so it is with man. Variety in all forms must be appreciated and honored. Behold the birds of the sky. Do the ravens war against the sparrow, or the sparrow against the hummingbird? Of course not. Each has their role.

Only with man is this not so. Why is it that prejudice and hatred are a part of your lives? You are all God's children and loved equally. To hate your brother or sister is an abomination to God. If you would be pure, you must put away these things. There is no place in the Kingdom of God for this. If you hate those of another race, country, or religion, it will keep you out of God's Kingdom. The Golden Rule must be obeyed by all. There are no exceptions. If you treat your brother of another race in a way that you would not wish to be treated, you have broken the rule.

Prejudice is rampant in your world and it grieves the Father greatly to see His children behave in this way. You started out as one family, so all are indeed your brothers and sisters. You have lost sight of this and taken your sibling rivalry to an extreme. It is not for you to decide which race, nationality, or religion, should live or die. Yet man has oppressed and domi-nated with his "righteous hatred" those who are different, and caused much suffering. God is not pleased. To disagree is no reason to hate. To be different is no reason to die. The rose does not hate the daisy. Each is beautiful in its own way, as are each of you.

How is it that you have strayed so far that you cannot recognize the spark of God in the eyes of your fellow man? Look past the color, past the culture, past the religion. Look deeper. Look into the soul. The soul is not black, or white, or yellow, or red. The soul is pure light. It chooses the color of the body, the country of birth, the religion and the culture for the purposes of spiritual growth. Because each soul is unique, its choices are unique. There are many paths to God, but only one way—the way of love. When someone departs on a journey, you wish them well. You say, "Have a good trip," or "Bon Voyage." Life is also a journey. It is a journey home to God. Can you not wish each other well on the path home?

Race, color, and religion are temporary and limited to your lifetime here on Earth. Only the soul abides forever. Therefore, I urge you, beloved children of the Father, to care for one another, and love one another as I have loved you. You cannot love God and hate your fellow man. If you truly love God, you will see the spirit of God in every person, every soul, every being. This then, is your goal—to allow God to heal you and fill your heart with His love and peace. Pray much for this, for yourself and all mankind. There can be no true peace until every heart is healed. Let the tyranny come to an end, for I, Lord Jesus, gave my life equally for all.

My mother is here now, and wishes to speak with you.

My dear children. I, Mother Mary, implore you with my tears

to stop this form of madness. Your hearts have turned to stone and you live and breathe hatred. Then you kneel and pray for God's help to destroy each other. Do you truly expect God to answer this prayer?

This, dear children, is how it works. When you pray, what you ask for another comes to you first. If you ask a blessing for another, you are blessed. If you ask to destroy another, you destroy yourself. Has not my Son told you to "Love your enemies, bless them, and pray for them." Hold fast to His teachings, for they nourish your soul. There is room on God's Earth for everyone. Where does man think he has the right to exterminate an entire race of people? It is God who has placed them here. The arrogance of man is indeed great. Go and create your own planet. Then you can decide who lives there. Until you can do this, you will have to share this beautiful Earth with the rest of God's children.

Soon the Kingdom of God will return to Earth, and many will stand outside weeping, for they will not be allowed in. They will have lost this golden opportunity because of hatred, prejudice, and violence. Give heed to my words and turn to God and the way of love while there is yet time. Do not delay to do this, for time is short. Extend the hand of friendship to all, no matter what color, race, religion, or nationality. A true child of God sees through the eyes of God. Let us pray together to heal the spirit of man. Jesus and I stand ready to assist you in this most important matter. We hold you in our hearts and prayers always.

The Lord Jesus and Mother Mary,
received by Romayne de Kanter

CHAPTER 25

ANIMALS

by
Saint Francis of Assisi

✠ ANIMALS ✠

PART I:

THE ANIMAL SPECIES

Greetings and gratitude to all animal lovers everywhere. This is the one you know as Saint Francis and today we will explore the world of animals.

Animals are not just "things." All animals have souls. All animals have personality. All animals are evolving through their experiences just as you are. Animals also have a collective spirit and a group soul that looks after each species as a whole. They have much wisdom to share with man, if man would but listen with his heart and with respect. All God's creatures deserve love and respect. These creatures have agreed to share this planet with you for the purposes of mutual benefit and evolvement. Many of them now regret that choice and are saddened by the lack of understanding on the part of humans.

In the beginning, man and animals were not enemies, but loving companions. When the spirit of abuse entered the world, all that changed. Man began to abuse himself, each other, as well as the animals, and the old ties of loyalty were severed. Man forgot the language of animals and the spirit of fear entered and made it worse. Then came greed, and what man did not slaughter out of fear, he did so out of greed.

The animals though, have remained in their pure state. Although wary of man (with good reason), they nevertheless remain ever ready to rekindle the original relationship with man.

Animals are a treasure and a delight to the Father. They are pure and without sin. They teach you to play, and the Master Jesus told you to "behold the birds of the air." They are always singing joyful songs of praise. They add much in the way of interest in your lives. Without the animals, you would be lost, for indeed they bring valuable knowledge to the Earth plane. This is much more than what you learn by observation. It also exists in the collective consciousness in the form of studies and knowledge that man gives himself credit for "discovering." In reality, those of the animal kingdom brought these truths with them as their gifts when they agreed to dwell here.

When a species becomes extinct, their collective spirit also leaves the planet and with it also goes the knowledge, their gift, to man. I hear many of you saying, "So what?" Oh, beloved souls, in your present state of mind you cannot conceive of the marvelous inventions lost through the removal of this wealth of knowledge! Dear ones, stop thinking of these as dumb animals. They are far from it. They are highly advanced group souls with high levels of technology.

Sonar came into your world through the bat. Even the ant is quite advanced. The bee with its knowledge of pollen, and even the hearing and sense of smell of the family dog are far greater than yours. The eagle can spot a tiny mouse from miles in the air. These things even you cannot do, no matter how hard you try, as you place yourself above these creatures. Even the humble virus has outsmarted you, which should tell you it is not as primitive as you might think.

The point is, beloved souls, that the animal kingdom, the plant kingdom—indeed all of God's Creation—are filled with wisdom and must be honored and respected, loved and blessed. All is made by the hand of the Father. To disrespect what God created is to disrespect God. He did not create for you to abuse, and abuse in all forms must end.

In God's perfect world there is only love. The ways of love are many, and man has barely scratched the surface. The Kingdom of God is the Kingdom of Love. This is how to tell if the Kingdom of God is truly within YOU.

Make friends with the wise and beautiful creatures who share Mother Earth with you. Speak to them with your heart, for the language of love is the universal language understood by all. It takes a long time to heal the effects of abuse. This is also true for animals. Animals do not hate, and have a hard time dealing with man's hatred, neglect, and indifference. We in the animal kingdom have much repair work to do when the animals return to spirit. This should not be.

Make room for God's creatures in your world. They have a right to exist the same as you. They have a right to their home and habitat. If someone barged into your home without permission, you would be somewhat upset. When you go into where they make their homes, speak to them in your heart and ask permission. Lack of respect is unwise and upsetting to everyone. There is a sacredness to all life that man has forgotten, and must be remembered and treated as such.

Ponder these words in your heart and become wise once again, lest nature herself turn upon you. There are consequences to all actions, some not so desirable. Destroy not the beauty of God's handiwork for your greed or pleasure, but lovingly care for it as befitting a child of the Most High.

I, St. Francis, offer you the wealth of my expertise with the little treasures of God, and extend God's peace to all.

Saint Francis of Assisi,
received by Romayne de Kanter

THE ANIMAL KINGDOM OF EARTH

Hello and greetings to all. This is Saint Francis of Assisi. I am here today to talk to you about the animals. As you know, I am the Patron Saint of Animals. So let's talk turkey, or should I say, let's talk about the turkeys and all the other wonderful, loving animals of your planet, our beloved Earth.

In the beginning, when this planet was created, God, our Father made a roster (as you would say) of all the animals who would dwell on this Earth. I wish to say this very strong statement. Every animal, large or small, plays an invaluable role in the ecology and balancing of this planet. When just one species becomes extinct then there is a *major* imbalance in the world of nature. Needless to say, Mother Earth is giving much effort to keep her bearings—to stay in balance. On a much more serious note, to this present day mankind has done much harm to his beloved partners who dwell with him on this planet. There is much suffering lived every day by these wonderful souls, the animals.

Allow me to give you some examples. These words may seem harsh; however, they are true. Some people beat and starve their dogs and cats. They abandon the young of domestic animals because they are a bother. People trap and kill animals for their coat of fur. People abuse animals by making them live in deplorable and inhumane conditions every day until they are old enough to slaughter for their fur. Animals are caged in tiny quarters and tortured daily for the purpose of research. These are just a few examples of the pain and suffering animals endure at the hand of man. Understand, beloved souls: these animals are part of God's vast Creation. God loves all His Creation, from every insect, reptile, rodent, bird, cat, dog, lion, tiger, all the way to the largest elephant. These animals are a part of God. When you harm an animal, you disrespect our Father God.

Now there are animals God, the Father, put on this Earth for the purposes of food for human consumption. These animals have this knowledge before going into the Earth plane. And the vast majority of these animals suffer greatly before they reach their final destination at the food processing plant. The majority of the meat that reaches your supermarket has been tainted with harmful chemicals. These animals live in conditions that God and nature never intended for them. Because of this they become sick from the abuse and must be given antibiotics and other pharmaceuticals so that they may live and do not pass the disease to humans. If man would understand that if he would turn to God for the solutions to these vast growing problems with the animal supply of food, he and all the animals and the world would benefit greatly. There is a *better way*—the way through God, the Father.

When man first inhabited this planet, man and animal were one. They lived together in total balance and harmony. There was great respect for one another. It saddens me to say this has changed greatly. In the beginning, man worked with the animals and the animals worked with man. There was communication between them in the beginning times. Animals are great teachers, healers, and givers of love. Do you notice when you are not feeling well, your dog will come to be with you? The dog is giving you healing and comfort. It is within their instinct and being to do so. The vibration they give to you is one that helps the colors of your aura to change to a more vibrant, healed color. The dog's vibration of love absorbs the negative colors of your aura and transmutes them into a more vibrant color. This will always happen if you will allow it. So be good to your dog and your dog will be good to you.

Every animal has a soul, a divine soul, that feels abuse and pain—and that soul also feels love and joy, and gives that love out. Many people think the animals are nothing, that human beings are much more important than animals. This is not true. God, our Father cherishes every animal who walks, crawls, slithers, flies, jumps, rolls, and swims across this great land of planet Earth. As God, the Father cherishes you, beloved ones, He also cherishes, loves, and adores His beloved animals.

You may not know this. However, I will tell you now. Every animal has great intelligence within its being. This intelligence is powerful knowledge from the universe. For example, many species of birds on this planet know when to fly south for the winter. No person told them to do this. They have this great knowing of when it is time to do so. Also there are many animals that can see in total darkness of the night. They can see through what you would term infrared night vision. These nocturnal animals can sense heat with their vision. These animals are born with this instilled within them. The beloved one who is writing these words that I am telling her, has often wondered what happens when an animal is hunted and killed by another animal for the purpose of feeding. This hunt may look brutal. However, it is not as it appears to you. When an animal is being hunted by another, that animal's soul reaches us in the animal kingdom *before* the animal is caught and killed. There is a physical reaction of the mind and body of that hunted animal that you see. That soul felt no pain. When an animal dies from abuse by the hand of man, that animal's soul *does* feel pain. The animal who dies by the hand of nature (whether it is from another animal for food or storms, floods, etc.) will adjust very well back into the animal kingdom. This is also true for the domestic animals who are loved and well taken care of by the people they live with. When they pass over into the animal kingdom they are happier souls who enjoyed their time on Earth. This is *not true* for the animals who die from abuse at the hand of man. These precious souls come back to God, the Father and all of us who do God's work in the animal kingdom, in a state of distress. These loving souls *need and are given* much healing and love for as long as needed.

Without God's precious gift of animals on planet Earth, human beings could not survive on this Earth plane. All animals are vital to you and Earth. All animals bring to you and planet Earth a great balancing of all ecological systems and great love and invaluable, highly evolved intelligence. If mankind were to communicate with God, our Father and express his desire to be at one with the animals—to live with animals in total harmony, to respect animals and make peace with them—mankind's life would be enriched beyond what words can express.

Understand, and please remember, you and the animals of this world are both part of God's loving Creation. Our Father God in Heaven would be so very pleased if all His children would do everything they can to be kind and respectful toward animals. For when you make peace with the animals, the animals will be peaceful toward you. This is the Law of the Land. Man has invaded many of the territories that animals have had for their homes for many, many years. Mankind has cleared away and restructured their habitat, forcing animals to place themselves in new and different areas which they can have a difficult time adapting to. All of the "small" things that are insignificant to man are not so insignificant to the universal Laws of Balance that God designed for this planet.

It is my pleasure to report that man has taken an active part in some organizations in this world that benefit the treatment and concern given to animals. In their combined efforts, these various organizations have saved the lives and habitats of millions of animals. These organizations that focus their attention on saving animals and the humane treatment of the animals not only serve God and the animal kingdom, they serve mankind as well. These organizations help to keep the animal world in balance, which greatly affects the world as you have come to know it. God sees every thing you do. You may think there is no one with you to witness or see what was done. However, beloved ones, God saw you. God knows your every move, your every thought.

Pray for your animals. It is really very simple. If the animals that you are caring for in your home do something that annoys you, then pray to God for help with that situation. For example, if your dog barks too often, then ask the Father God in Heaven for help to train him in a humane manner. God will answer your prayer. Call upon me, Saint Francis. I will always bring to you knowledge that will benefit both you and the animal. If you beat your animals, you will cause their souls great pain. The solution to any problem is through God. Both God and I will bring to your life, understanding to take care of any situation involving animals with an easy solution that is of no harm to you or the animal. If you love and respect the animals, they will love and respect you. God did not bring animals into the Earth so that they would do harm to man, and God never intended man to do harm to them. Throughout many years, man's connection with God has weakened. Because of this, mankind's connection with the animals of Earth has been, for the majority, weakened greatly. When you strengthen your connection with God, then fear—all fear—will not play such a strong role in your life. Without the fear of animals, you can begin to make peace with them. When you are One with God and have the strongest connection with Him, you shall have no fear of any animal at any time. When you are One with God, the Father, you can look into the eyes of any animal and see the great love of God inside their souls. I send you peace and love from the great animal kingdom.

Saint Francis of Assisi,
received by Eve Barbieri

PART 3:

ON THE SUBJECT OF DOGS

Many greetings to all. This is Saint Francis of Assisi. I wish to speak to you about dogs. Every dog on this Earth is loved and cherished by God, the Father, every angel, and every spirit being who works in the animal kingdom. Also, every Ascended Master and all the Forces of Light who serve the Lord our God, love, cherish and help welcome dogs back to the animal kingdom or to the spirit plane to be with the loving spirit beings they have known during their Earth life. Every dog and puppy is important to God. They are not considered "nothing" to God. God, our Father does not regard any of His Creation as nothing. Dogs are to be treated with love and respect, for they are God's dogs also.

At this time I wish to give you some information on what the excessive breeding of dogs has done to this animal species. As I have said earlier, mankind and animals once worked together in harmony on planet Earth. This is true for all animals—the bears, the lion, and of course the wolf, or wild dog. As you may know, over the course of many eons (thousands of years) mankind has manipulated and tampered with the breeding of these wild dogs. This was mostly done for a specific purpose. For example, some Chinese dogs were bred to be aggressive. This was for the purpose of guarding their religious temples and their temples of royalty. Another example would be the bloodhound and the basset hound, as well as many other breeds that were altered from their original wolf or wild dog form for the purpose of hunting—all different types of hunting. Some people have bred the already different species of dogs to create dogs of beauty and for different sizes, to cuddle in their arms and to create long legs for the purpose of racing and recreation.

You may ask why some dogs are aggressive and mean, and other dogs are the opposite of this—they are kind, loving, and gentle. There are various reasons why this is. Allow me to give you some enlightenment. The main reason why domestic dogs are aggressive and mean is because of the improper breeding of these animals. This is called inbreeding. Certain people who breed these dogs do this in an immoral manner, which goes against God's laws of nature. They force these dogs to reproduce or procreate in an incestuous manner, time and time again. This is usually done for the purposes of greed. When dogs are deeply inbred, this changes the brain chemistry of the animal. This inbreeding causes the mechanisms in their brain to become extremely off-balance—unnatural. You see, beloved ones, these dogs do not breed this way in the wild. They do not procreate in an incestuous manner. Dogs in the wild know this by instinct. However, when held in captivity, and by mankind's manipulations, these instincts the domestic dogs possess become confused and distorted. I must make understood that not all breeders of domestic dogs follow this immoral practice. There are many who follow the laws of nature. And then there are some people who breed these domestic dogs and use many immoral, cruel and unethical practices to manipulate and change God's perfect laws of nature. The making of money is usually the motive behind these wrongful dog-breeding practices.

Another reason for a domestic dog's cruel nature is due to mankind's abuse. As we have said in this book, all of God's Creation needs, deserves, and is to be given respect and love.

This law stands true for all people and all animals. Understand, beloved souls, dogs (as well as all God's animals) have an aura—an energy field which surrounds them.

Dogs also have four specific embodiments. They have, like humans have, a mental body, a physical body, an emotional body, and a spiritual body. In human beings, when severe abuse is given, this harm affects all embodiments of this human. The same is true for dogs. When people abuse dogs by hitting them, beating them, or any other harmful acts, this action will change the molecular structure of the dog's brain. Abuse causes a dog to become confused and fearful. Many times abuse is given to puppies or young dogs. What this does is cause their brains to develop abnormally. This causes the young dog's mind to think in a distorted manner, which will many times cause the dog to act in a defensive way later in its life, and sometimes these dogs will act in a defensive way for no reasonable cause. Their young minds have been programmed to defend themselves against any form of abuse.

Understand, beloved ones, dogs do not understand why they are being beaten or abused. Understand that they have instilled in their brain a mechanism to fight for survival. And during the times of abuse, these mechanisms and connections in their brains fail to function in the proper manner—the God-given manner. Remember, God is the opposite of abuse. When these mechanisms and connections in the dog's brain malfunction, then the animal can and does at times act in a distorted, defensive way. There is no reason ever to abuse or harm dogs. If your dog has behavioral challenges, then, beloved souls, take the responsibility to do what is best for your dog. Invest in some dog-training classes. These classes teach the dog and person who cares for the dog to train the animal in a humane and loving manner that gives much praise and attention. Love teaches with God-power. Abuse teaches only fear.

There is also another reason for the domestic dog's aggressive action that I, Saint Francis, wish to reflect on. That is the use of chemicals. As you are all very aware of, there is nothing pure and clean on this planet at this time. Pollution is a very hazardous problem in your world. The air is polluted greatly. The food of today is impure and unclean. However, the most polluted resource on planet Earth today is the drinking water. It would be very wise for all people of Earth to pray for their water supply to be blessed and made pure by the cleansing and purifying Light of God, the Holy Father in Heaven. This prayer (said often) will prevent any chemicals in the water from being harmful to the physical body.

Understand, beloved souls, when you consider these three major resources for survival on your planet, you must consider the vast amount of pollution that exists in these resources. There are tons of pollutants in the air you breathe. The food that people and domestic dogs eat is laden with chemicals such as food additives, artificial flavors and colors, and numerous chemical preservatives. Some of the commercial dog food companies use unclean fillers, additives, and harmful preservatives in the dog food they produce. Certain breeds of dogs and some dogs individually are sensitive to these chemicals in the food they eat and the water they drink. The anatomy of a canine was not designed by God to endure such constant exposure to these man-made chemicals. These various chemicals cause mental disturbances in the brains of some dogs. These strange, unclean, and impure chemicals can cause the brain chemistry of a dog to change, therefore allowing the dog to act in an unnatural manner.

Also there are some people who want their guard dogs to be as mean and aggressive as possible. Some of these people train their dogs to be this way. Others will intentionally give their dogs very harmful chemicals, which are known to make the dog's mindset extremely unstable. One of these devastatingly harmful chemicals is the powder human beings put in the bullets of their guns—gunpowder. The use of gunpowder and other mind-altering chemicals such as mind-altering and stimulating drugs cause the dog's mind to be in total insanity. The dog is insane when given these terrible, harmful substances. The dog no longer has control over its thoughts and actions. The dog only knows to attack. The dog truly suffers greatly when these chemicals and drugs are induced by people who wish their dogs to be extremely mean and aggressive, or when people wish to harm their dogs.

Understand, beloved ones, God created every animal on Earth. God is pure love and only creates love. People of the Earth, through free will and free choice, can change God's Creation of love into something that is thought to be feared. The canine species was created on Earth to bring enlightenment, love, and happiness for all to enjoy. If you wish to bring a loving dog into your home, ask God, the Father or I, Saint Francis, to guide you to the most suitable dog. The rewards of having one of these delightful, loving animals in your home are too numerous to mention.

Beloved souls, always know that if you take good care of your dog, the dog in return will fill your heart with immeasurable love and joy. I hope these words have brought to you a greater understanding of these precious and endearing creatures of God's wonderful and miraculous animal kingdom. With light and love to you from our God, the Father, I thank you for hearing these words.

Saint Francis of Assisi,
received by Eve Barbieri

CHAPTER 26

THE CHILDREN

by
Mother Mary

THE CHILDREN

Part 1:

MIND DEVELOPMENT OF CHILDREN

Greetings of love and joy. This is Mother Mary, mother of Jesus.

I wish to bring you some information and knowledge about the children of your world. Children have a special place in the heart of God. They also hold a special light in my heart as well. Children are the world's most precious gift. They are given to you by God, the Creator of the Heavens. Without children there would be no future. Do you see how precious they are? Your entire future on this planet revolves around the children more than any other resource. Your children are invaluable. Your money, monetary system, and precious metals hold some significance in the future, but it is the children who hold the most importance.

When you love a child—unconditionally love a child—from when it is an infant, and pass no judgments on it before it is at a reasonable age in its life, then that love is carried on throughout the duration of its life. When a small child is abused, the child has his/her heart broken to the point where there are holes and tears in the aura. The ill feeling inside of it affects its self-worth and he/she does harm to itself and to others. The harm they do has somewhat of a domino effect. They harm others and the others will go to harm others, and so on. Understand, when a child is small, the mind and thoughts are extremely fragile at this time. Their self-worth, their thoughts of themselves, are very vulnerable. Abuse given to a child at this time can be, and is very damaging to their young lives.

Think of your child's mind and all children's minds as a place where there are the most beautiful, fragile, tiny glass sculptures. And think of abuse as a big, speeding truck that breaks and damages all these beautiful tiny glass sculptures into pieces. Any abuse will do great harm to a child's mind, be it physical abuse, emotional abuse, mental abuse, or sexual abuse. The traumatic effect of abuse lasts for a very long time in their mindset. Their thoughts and opinions of themselves are tarnished. And they, the wonderful precious children, will find themselves longing for the love and praise they so need and desire for years to come. As they get older, they may (and usually do) seek out certain people or a person who will give them the emotional satisfaction they feel they need to become fulfilled. This is the cause for many children to stray away from their families and their homes. The love and nurturing they sought as a child was non-existent in their young life, so they now will go and seek out the ones who will bring them the emotional fulfillment they so desire and need in order to feel whole again. The person or people the young ones seek, in order to bring themselves into a *one*, a complete feeling inside of them, are usually the ones who tear them apart even more. This is very distressing to God, the Father in Heaven.

Since free will is always invoked, there is not much that we, the Ascended Masters and angels, can do to stop this. Many young people are returned to us in the spirit world and are confused as to what happened to them. They do not understand the betrayal. There is much help and healing given to them at this time, to bring them back into God's love and into God's loving hands.

Understand, dear ones, it is the love that blossoms from the heart which brings to the children and others total, complete wholeness into their being. You may ask how so many of the young people have turned so violent and mean inside. This is due to the conditioning of the mind when they were young. There are many sources for this influence. For instance, the parents' prejudice and hatred within their own hearts is taught and instilled into their children's minds when they are very young and impressionable. The next and most influential is the television set. Break apart the word tele-vision. These are visions that others are telling you. The people who put these certain visions on the television that are of a violent nature are ones who enjoy doing evil.

In the early times, it was understood that moviegoers were shocked when there were mean and horrible acts depicted on the screen. This was a sort of fascination—that people could watch this happening from start to finish. And as you know, this fascination made large sums of money for the filmmakers. This of course, carried itself over onto the television screen where very young children see these evil acts portrayed over and over. Understand, beloved ones, children starting from a very young age, are taught by example. When you say the letter "A," they will try to say the letter "A," and so on. When they watch violent acts, they will imitate these acts. When you teach a child to tie his own shoes, he or she will watch you do it first; then they will tie their shoes for themselves. I am attempting to bring into the realization that what the children see, whether it is in reality or on a television screen or movie screen, they will do the same.

The same principle holds true for music. The words and tones of certain music have the same damaging effects on the brains and minds of children as the violence and hatred seen on the movie screen and television screen. Certain music tones are negative music tones and what these tones do is suppress the brain function. This suppression is damaging to the aura. It allows the aura to break up. This action crushes a child's defense against harm done unto himself/herself. The words leave the child who is listening to these evil words, without any defense to protect himself/herself from being programmed by what the lyrics say. This is tragic for the child's mindset. Their thoughts of themselves, others, and the world can be (and usually are) changed for their entire lifetime as that person. Unfortunately, this change is not a good thing that will enhance their life and bring them closer to God and true happiness. This is a detrimental change that will keep them away from God by their own mindset, by the programming of the music. I, Mother Mary, mother of Jesus, ask you to please pay attention to the music, television shows, and video games your children are involved with. Their mind is so very precious.

The most hazardous influence of all are the video games that are on the market today. These games actually allow the child to interact with the violence. This brings the knowledge to the child that this is what *they* did. These violent acts are what *they* have accomplished. They are rewarded by the most murders, by winning the game, or by scoring the most points. This tricks their mind into believing in total acceptance of these violent acts of hatred. This allows them to think this is fun, that this— to do these terrible acts of violence—is a normal way of life. Understand: some children will spend hours playing these violent games. Much damage to their sense of reality is done during that time. They are hypnotized by these machines, and the child's concept of reality is changed. Not only are the violent acts portrayed on these video machines allowed, they are fun and rewarding. The child's mind is programmed after playing these games. Their sense of right or wrong, good or evil, is completely distorted. The child's feeling and sense of compassion and good will are desensitized, leaving that wonderful God-given part of them numb inside.

If you are a loving and concerned parent, take an active role by monitoring what your children may do for entertainment. You can begin to change the course of their life for the better.

I thank you for hearing these words. My love to you.

Mother Mary, mother of Jesus,
received by Eve Barbieri

THE SELF-IMAGE OF CHILDREN

Greetings, my dear children. This is Mother Mary, and I am here to deliver a message for parents and those who care for the children. There is a tremendous lack of self-esteem among today's youth, much more than in the past. You might say it has been "handed down" from parent to child. When the parent or caregiver has low self-esteem, they do not know how to build the child's image in a positive way. There are many good and helpful books available on this subject. You can find them in your local library.

The self-image is of importance in that it allows a person to grow and develop to their full potential. This is not a false pride that puts one above their fellow man. Rather, it uplifts each of you to see your true worth. Each person has a gift to share with the world. The sharing of this gift raises your self-esteem, for in giving you also receive.

Little children bring gifts to you and to each other also. It is important to see the uniqueness in each child—the personality and characteristics. In some cultures, the child is not given a name until these unique characteristics have become apparent, and then the child is given a name that is appropriately chosen to accurately describe them. This may sound strange to you until you try it for yourself. Suppose you are a nurse, and your name was "Angel of mercy." Self-esteem would no longer be an issue for you. Everyone now knows who you are and what your gift is. Now of course, not every nurse can have this same name, nor should they claim to. Some nurses could be named, "Shows no mercy," but then, would that not be helpful to you as a patient? The point is, dear souls, when you see the budding and flowering of a gift within a child, think of a phrase that describes this gift and use this phrase to focus your attention in this area of their growth, for it will determine who they are and what they are about in this world.

Always focus on the positive—on the gift from God that came here with them. Even the "Shows no mercy" nurse may be a "Cooks with love" and should have been a food caterer. This kind of phrase can become like a middle name, such as Donna, writer of poems, who may someday become an author, or William, defender of the small, who may become a lawyer or policeman. Often, in the past, the last name of a person denoted their gift or talent—such as Carpenter or Baker. When you know who you are and what you are about—when you know what your talents and gifts are, there is a sense of self-fulfillment and honor. You have a sense of direction in life. A child who has been given the gift of praise and nurturing of their God-given talents will not need to look elsewhere to "find themselves."

Recognize the gifts your children have and encourage their development. Encourage creativity, and praise lavishly. Do not criticize. Perhaps your way of doing something is not the only way it can be done, and you too can learn. Be careful with your words. You would be hurt if someone called you stupid. You would be hurt even more if it came from someone you loved. And so, beloved souls, do not wound your children. To destroy a child's self-esteem in this way can take many lifetimes to repair. Let the Golden Rule be your guide in all that you say and do. Teach by example, and always with praise. A child may not do a task perfectly in the beginning. To go and redo it yourself tells them they couldn't do it good enough to please you. Now, what is more important, a child's self-esteem, or a perfectly made bed? As a child gains confidence and satisfaction in a job well done (even if it isn't perfect), the rewards you will reap for your patience and kindness will amaze you.

Children who are praised and valued do not need to seek these things in gangs and drugs. Children have unlimited potential. In whatever capacity you work with them, you can make a tremendous difference in their lives. They are little people who will become your future doctors, scientists, and employers, and they are your finest investment. Many parents have made poor choices and traded broken hearts and broken lives for their fine houses and lifestyle. True happiness is not found in the abundance of material things. Many lives are wasted and sacrificed on the altars of materialism. Do not neglect the precious souls of God in the pursuit of wealth. A big, beautiful house that is cold and lonely is no refuge in the storms of life. A small, cozy cottage filled with love and laughter is. Look within your heart and pray always for true wisdom and guidance.

I, Mother Mary, have spoken to you on behalf of the little children who are in your lives and in your care. It is my wish to see happy children once again, and dear souls, there are very few of these anymore. Please do what you can to help change this sad situation. My blessings and help are with each of you.

Mother Mary, mother of Jesus,
received by Romayne de Kanter

CHAPTER 27

GODLY SUFFERING

by
The Holy Spirit/The Great White Brotherhood of God

✤ GODLY SUFFERING ✤

Greetings and much love to all. This is the Holy Spirit, the Great White Brotherhood of God. At this time, we would like to give some enlightenment on the subject of "Godly suffering."

We wish to say, so that you can understand, "Godly Suffering" is a sacrificial suffering in service to God's will. It is different from the pain that the vast majority of people suffer from every day, which is caused mostly by karma and poor choices. There has been much, much killing and disrespect to the human beings of Earth in the past thousands of years. Karma, believe it or not, is a teacher—a great teacher—for full understanding and knowing, so that history doesn't keep repeating itself. It balances the scales so that the experience can be marked off the books, or may we say, the Akashic (past life) Record. It is a form of restitution. Through pain and suffering, both yours and others, you grow (evolve) rapidly. You grow spiritually.

However, when one is in service to God, the Father in Heaven, and is put into the position of suffering, that person has the white light of God and the Christ light around them at all times. Understand, beloved souls, the souls who have chosen to come here with God's purpose and God's will in their life's plan—they have (at all times) the white light of God flowing through their veins. The love of God and His white light surrounds and encompasses every fiber, every cell, of their body, and illuminates every fiber of light in their soul. This keeps their mind in God-mind. When one's mind is in God-mind, that person has total and complete strength and love given to them every minute of every day. This frees them from fear and from the kind of pain that is felt by human beings who are not in service to God. Understand, what is felt by the ones who are in service is still what you would term pain. However, it is a different pain. It is a pain in the service of love. Love, the feeling, the emotion, the service of love, is one of a very high vibration. People who serve God's love, who have their heart in love, dwell on this planet on a much higher vibration. The higher your vibration, the more highly attuned you are to feeling God's love, which changes the pain felt during suffering. During the times of pain to the body, there are legions of forces of light delivering healing and love from God to that being. Jesus received some of the most powerful healing ever given to anyone on the planet Earth. God did not abandon him, nor was the connection between Jesus and God ever lost in any way.

Jesus volunteered to come down to the Earth to be the greatest teacher of all. He knew before he came that there would be great harm done to him. People have free will and free choice. Teachings beyond what you could imagine came from that time and affected thousands upon thousands of people for thousands of years afterward. He knew He would be sacrificed due to the dense thoughts and actions on the planet at that time. Do you see how they didn't really take Him? He ascended into the heavens so you could know that it is possible for you to do that (ascend) as well. There was tremendous teaching done at that time. What happened to Jesus was not pleasing to God. God gives us, all of us, free will. It is His precious gift to us. He is not a controlling God.

God's love is the most powerful force in this universe and all universes. It is pure light. When you hold God's love in your heart, as the ones who suffer in service to God do, then you hold pure light within your being. The ones who hold pure light, God's pure light, never lose their connection with God, the Father. This strong connection will keep them in the midst of God's wondrous blessings always. No person, no army of people, no amount of wealth, can take this—God's love and blessings—away from them at any time. The love they—the ones who are in service to God and only God, the Father—feel from God as they walk on this planet is love beyond what you could ever imagine. Understand dear ones, the ones who serve God and only God and God's light—not money, not their own pleasures—have given themselves into God's love. They have total trust and faith in God. This action opens and keeps strong the connection to God, the Father. When you have a total connection with God, when you are one with God, when you live by God's laws, God holds your soul in His protection. Your soul is in God's pure white light at all times, even in the trials of pain and suffering that many may inflict upon you. Always remember, man has free will and free choice. However, supernatural strength is given to all who suffer for righteousness sake.

God, creator of this universe and all universes, never abandons anyone, and God never abandons the ones who come to this planet to bring an understanding, to educate mankind, and to make a difference by being the example that many will remember for many times to come.

We give our love to you always.

The Great White Brotherhood of God,
received by Eve Barbieri

CHAPTER 28

SIN

by
The Holy Spirit/The Great White Brotherhood of God

✛ SIN ✛

Greetings of joy and love, dear beloved ones. The Heavens are at your grasp. But most of you believe you are not worthy of such greatness and holiness because you have sinned, and some have sinned a great sin against God and themselves. You must understand, sin is here in your land to teach you. Without the choice to sin, your life would not be so full of the knowledge you have. God knows there is sin. God loves you, regardless of your sins. That is not to say He is pleased by your sins. However, God is pleased when you have learned from your sins and have turned away from your sins in the past and turn to Him for love, forgiveness, and to redeem yourself—and have the desire and willingness to be one with Him. You are worthy to have your sins forgiven by God, the Father. You are worthy of being loved and forgiven by the Lord of Hosts—God, our Father. Many people—most people—believe they are never going to be forgiven, and they are going to burn in the Lake of Fire or go to Hell—that God is an angry God. So they think, "What is the use? Why should I even try?" They fear God; they think that God, the Father hates them for who they are and what they have done. Nothing, my dear beloved ones, can be further from the truth. You are, have always been, and will always be loved totally, 100%—loved by God, the Father in the Heavens. This is absolute 100% truth, undisputed truth.

Life is a joy. It is to be cherished, not feared. Love is the most desired feeling among humans. Every one of you wish to be loved and yet you turn away from the one Source, the Source most holy, the one and only God who loves you at every minute of every day of your eternal life, without fail. We wish to bring you out of this consciousness—of thinking you are

271

hated and damned by God. Nothing could be further from the truth. The churches and religions of this day and age literally prey on the ignorance of mankind's mindset and leads them to believe that if you do not do what they say in *their beliefs*, then you are in big trouble with God, the Father; that you are in rebellion to Him; that your life will change for the worse and you will be cursed by God. This is nothing but fear in action in the hearts and minds of the men and women who lead others—many, many others to believe this way of thinking.

Understand, God's relationship with you—God's religion—is love and only love. Not to persecute or damn, but to love you and hold you safe in His loving arms forever. All of you, every one of you on this planet is worthy of this. God can forgive anything. God can fix anything and make it whole and pure in God's love and light. God can and does heal anything and everything. You see, it is your own mind that traps you, that keeps you in fear and away from God's love. You are so very loved by God and so very important to Him. God, the Father, knows your every thought, every action, and every emotion. God is always with you. Please know in your hearts and in your minds that you are loved by God. You are deserving and worthy of this. God, the Father, will never ever turn Himself away from you at any time. Please know this. God is love—pure, 100% white light love. Darkness does not dwell in the consciousness of God. Love is God and God is love.

To know this truly, without doubt, is true bliss. To have no fear where God is concerned, in your mind and in your hearts, is, as you would say on Earth, Heaven. The "Kingdom of Heaven" is within you. Jesus said this two thousand years ago in the Sermon on the Mount. This truth is an eternal truth. You are created by God. You are one with God. To go within to seek the Kingdom of God means simply to be still, be quiet, and have your mind take you to the heavens—to be still, to concentrate one on one with God and with His energy, to know that inside your mind you are sitting next to God.

God loves you. God is not going to ever raise His hand to you, scold you, yell at you, or send you to hell as you have been told in the past. God would be so very happy for His children to come sit with Him so that God may heal you and love you always. Understand, you must go to God for healing and love. If you do not bring yourself to Him, then you cannot feel His love or energy. God does not impose Himself on you. He does not control your choices. Your will is yours. We would however, like to stress the importance of using your will and inner peace and love in alignment with God, our Father.

Your life, your eternal life, is a precious gift from God, to be cherished. All life is created by God and is to be respected and dignified. Your life is dignified by God. God loves you and you are forever worthy of His love. Respect yourself, love yourself. Know where you are on your spiritual path. Understand you are evolving. You are growing with knowledge and wisdom. Your thoughts are yours. They belong to you and reflect what you do and who you are. You must realize when you go within to seek God, your thoughts become joined in God's love and energy. This will purify your thoughts to bring your thoughts into a higher consciousness. What you tell yourself, what you speak—the words you say to yourself and others—also has a profound effect on your life and your spiritual level of consciousness. To be positive, always positive, about yourself and situations that may be challenging will raise your consciousness and your intellect. This will always much better suit your life than to look at yourself, others, and situations in a negative way. The negative emotions and judgments will only hold you back and keep you from being one with the Creator God, by keeping you locked in fear. Fearful emotions are very damaging to the psyche. They hold you by controlling your emotions and lock you into a defeatist attitude that is very difficult (by the position of your own mindset) to break free from. Prayer to God, the Holy Father in Heaven, is the only way to break free from this negative thought pattern. Through prayer you will be free from fear and from the ill thoughts that are associated with fear, one being the thought that you are not worthy of God's love. You are and will always be worthy of God's love. This is truth—Divine Truth.

We would like to thank you for your attention on this subject, since it is very near and dear to our hearts that you find God in your own heart and accept His love for yourself. Open up your mind, your heart, and your life to God without fear, for you are always loved without fail by God the Creator of this universe and all universes.

Our love to all the Children of God.

The Great White Brotherhood of God,
received by Eve Barbieri

CHAPTER 29

EVIL

by
The Holy Spirit/The Great White Brotherhood of God

✣ EVIL ✣

Greetings beloved. We, the Brotherhood of God, the Holy Spirit, rejoice in your interest in our words and messages. We who serve the Father and the Christ encourage you to continue your quest for knowledge and enlightenment. There is much more that all of us wish to teach you as you are ready and willing to absorb it. We shall never abandon you, for you walk with us and with God as you work with us in these ways, and all of heaven is here to help you. You will advance greatly in spirit as you move through these lessons. This is for your benefit in this life and beyond.

Today we wish to give you some insight on evil. Evil is most prevalent in your world at this time. Today people live more by the Seven Deadly Sins than by the Ten Commandments. This, dear ones, is evil. To place yourself in the company of evil puts you into a trap which is often difficult to escape from. Where there is greed, envy, pride, lust, gluttony, hatred, sloth, and the like, evil dwells. These are not called deadly sins for no reason. They are destroyers of souls. Remove yourself from this atmosphere, for it does not serve your highest good. Guard your precious soul from these things, and rebuke them as the Christ did.

Know, beloved children of God, that these sins can trick you if you are not careful. They tell you, "A little lust is okay," "You have been wronged, so it's justified to hate," and "one more for the road" is the friendly thing to do. With their lies they gain control over you more and more. You must be ever aware. Keep your thoughts pure and holy. Learn to forgive quickly. There is no such thing as a "little" hate, or a "little" lust, or a "little" evil. Evil is evil, and good is good. Surround yourself with goodness—good people, good activities, good thoughts, and your life will be good. Do good for others when you are in a position to do so. When you are not able to help in that moment, pray for the person in need and their situation. This is how to walk with God in love on a daily basis.

Do not be judgmental and condemn others for their weaknesses or choices. This is not your place and there but for the Grace of God go you also. The Christ came not to condemn the captives, but to free them. Pray for these trapped souls that they may find their way back to God. Do not look down on them and think you are holier than they. Be grateful that God has mercifully delivered you from a similar fate. You see beloved souls, spiritual pride is also evil. Remember the lesson that Jesus gave about the man who boasted in the temple of how good he was. Take heed that you do not do this, even in your heart.

Walk softly upon the Earth and let your light shine, your prayers be many, and your love be strong. Be gentle with yourself and others. Bless all things and all circumstances. Seek God's will and not your own. Your Father truly does know best. Go into the temple of your heart for all your guidance and answers. Ask, and you shall receive.

We, the Holy Spirit of God, the angels and saints, and the Father Himself join with the Christ to bless you as you thirst for righteousness, and ever await your call to assist you. May the peace of God rest in your soul.

The Great White Brotherhood of God
received by Romayne de Kanter

CHAPTER 30

GOD SPEAKS

by
Our Heavenly Father

✢ GOD SPEAKS ✢

PART 1:

A MESSAGE TO MY CHILDREN

Greetings to my precious children. This is your Father in Heaven, and I wish to speak to each of you today about our relationship.

I AM not dead, nor am I asleep. I AM fully aware of every one of my precious children. I hold you tenderly in my heart. My only desire is for your good. I gave you life—eternal life. When you were but a tiny spark of life, I loved you. Do not doubt my love and concern for you. Do not think anyone is more important to me than you, because you think they are smarter, or richer, or better in some way. Each of you is special in your own unique way—and loved for who you are, a very dear child of mine. My arms await you. You need never be afraid to approach me, for I will never harm you, no matter what you've heard. I will never turn my back on you. You are ever and always in my love.

You may forget about me, especially when things are going well in your life. But I never forget about you. I AM always there for you and await only your call and invitation to be a part of your life, but I shall never force myself upon you.

It is important for you to know me and how I feel about you. I AM not sitting "up there" waiting for you to make a mistake so I can "zap" you. I AM waiting for you to call so I can help you. It saddens me to see you in fear of me for no reason. I love you, no matter what, and always will. Let yourself be loved. You are standing in your own way. I AM reaching out to you. Take my hand and allow me to be a Father to you.

I have provided for all your needs, but you must remember to ask before they can come to you. Yes, I can read your thoughts and your heart. I know. You complain, but you fail to ask. I will not intervene unless you ask me to. I respect your choices, even those that cause you pain.

Each of you is very precious to me. Never doubt my love for you. Trust in it and depend on it. It is constant and will never fail. You are never alone, for I AM always with you, closer than you can imagine.

Today I wish to give you this reassurance. If you listen with your heart, you will hear me speaking these words directly to you. They are living words that will light up your heart and fill it with joy.

You do not need to go searching for me. I AM not lost. I'm right here with you. Allow me to comfort you, to teach you, and to care for you.

I AM only a prayer away, and I will always answer. You will find me in the stillness of your heart and mind. Take time to be quiet and hear my voice. Then you shall know perfect peace.

I, your Heavenly Father, pour out my blessings upon you, my dear children. Receive these blessings that I bestow on you from the throne of love, and walk with me.

Our Heavenly Father,
received by Romayne de Kanter

MENTAL ILLNESS

Greetings, my beloved children. I AM your Heavenly Father, your Creator, who is loving you every moment as I hold you in my heart. I have come today to this oracle because I see so many of you heartsick about your loved ones who have various forms of what you term, mental illness.

The brain, a component of the body, is physical, and as such can break down and deteriorate. This is a natural condition with all living things that exist in the physical world, and it is one that you fear. You fear it because you think that it is the sum total of you, and on Earth this is all you know. However, dear children, you are much more than a physical body and a brain. You are spirit, and you are only on Earth so you can experience a physical universe. Spirit cannot be contained within a physical body. Spirit is always free. When the brain does not function properly due to trauma or disease, it causes behaviors that are distressing to the loved ones and other observers. The person may not seem to know you, or remember how to complete simple tasks. In severe cases there may be coma. You feel you have somehow lost your loved one and you mourn.

Understand beloved souls, you—the real you, the spirit that you truly are—can never be lost. The Earth plane is one of illusion, and what you see is only a small part of the big picture. Within truth there is understanding, so allow me to explain.

You have perhaps heard the term, "As above, so below." This is truth, and the physical world and its activities of life mirror the spirit world. Now when a child is born, it is attached to its mother by an umbilical cord. And so it is that there exists a spiritual umbilical cord which connects your spirit body to your physical body. At death, this cord is severed and the spirit is free to return home. Now when the physical body is in coma, or no longer remembers who they are and cannot care for themselves, their spirit leaves the body. They do not have to endure pain and suffering unless they themselves choose to do so for the purpose of spiritual growth. This umbilical cord is quite a long one, and enables the spirit to go great distances, speak to other beings, such as angels and guides, and have many wonderful experiences, while they are still attached to their bodies. As long as their cord is attached, the life force continues to flow and enables the body to sustain life. It can appear as though the body is suffering and in great anguish. This is what you term as cellular memory, or automatic responses of the body to various stimuli. Since the person can enter and leave the body at will, they do not have to experience this unless they choose to do so. Let me stress that the body, no matter what state it is in, must be treated with kindness and respect, for my life force remains within it.

You see, my children, it is all about love. On Earth and in spirit, the lesson is always about love. The many aspects of love, the many dimensions of love, the unlimited power of love, is what it is all about. You ask the question in your songs, "What's it all about?" The answer, dear souls, is love. It's all about love. Do you understand? It is all about love and only about love. All of your experiences come to you to teach you some aspect of love. **Love is eternal and love cannot be lost.** These beings who choose to go through the experiences of mental illness have agreed to become teachers of compassionate love, allowing you to have this experience to develop this love within you. It is their gift to you. Pray always to see past the appearances, past the illusion, to the true reality and to learn the lessons of love it is trying to teach you.

Many have abandoned their loved ones and have lost this opportunity for much learning and advancement of their souls. But rest assured, dear ones, that the experiences will come to you again and again until the lesson is learned. In spirit, as in Earth school, you must pass the test in order to graduate to the next level of learning.

And so, beloved children, be at peace in your heart. Concentrate on learning the many ways of love and not on the appearances of pain and distress. If you pray, I will guide you and comfort you. My blessings are upon each of you and my love abides with you forever.

Our Heavenly Father,
received by Romayne de Kanter

PART 3:

RELIGION

With my Divine Love to all my children, this is God, your Heavenly Father. I am coming through to speak to you about religion and your worship of me.

All who worship me in the name of Love will receive salvation from me. THIS IS MY LAW. You are not to persecute or damn any of my children for their belief in me. For I AM God, and I know your every thought before it is known to you. I know and have record of every cell, atom, and molecule of every child of the human race on planet Earth. There are many paths to me, and my son Jesus Christ has paved each and every path, for He is the way to me. My son Jesus Christ is the way-shower to my kingdom. This is true for ALL religions, whether it is believed or not. My son Jesus Christ paved these golden paths of light to the Heavenly Kingdom before He came to the world and sacrificed Himself in the name of peace.

You are my children, my family, my true love. Go throughout your world and love and respect all who worship me. This is to be done regardless of the difference in religious beliefs, for I know what is in your soul. Do not war against your brother and sister because they are on a different spiritual path to me. Love your brothers and your sisters, for you are all a part of me. Ask for my blessings to all nations, for all colors of skin, and for all religious beliefs. You are all my Creation, and every religion that worships my love for all the world, for all the people of the world, and for all that lives in this world, will surely lead through the gates of my heavenly Kingdom. My love is given to all who know me and love me in their heart and soul.

My Kingdom, the Kingdom of God, is within each and every soul of my Creation. All who call to me with purity in their hearts are allowed to enter this Heavenly Kingdom. This is my law, the Law of Divine Love and Light to all. I AM THAT I AM.

Our Heavenly Father,
received by Eve Barbieri

PART 4:

LOVE LETTER FROM GOD

This is your Father, God in Heaven. I wish to speak to you today about Love. All of my Creation is made of Love—pure Divine Love. I love all of my children, every single one who lives on this planet and in all worlds. I love all of you with all of the Divine Power of Love that exists infinitely. You are my cherished ones, my very beloved. I love you now at this present moment and will for all time. I have given all of my children eternal life and eternal love. I have blessed you with a powerful and loving planet to be your host. I am with you always. I am within every cell, every molecule, every atom of your being. I will dwell in your hearts and minds only if I am asked to do so. You will always have free will and free choice invoked in your life. I will never control my children. I love you too much to ever hold you under my power. The power of all Divine Love in the universe is yours if you will choose to be one with me. All you must do is *ask*. I love every one of my children with the most powerful force of love in all of my Creation. I AM THAT I AM.

Our Heavenly Father,
received by Eve Barbieri

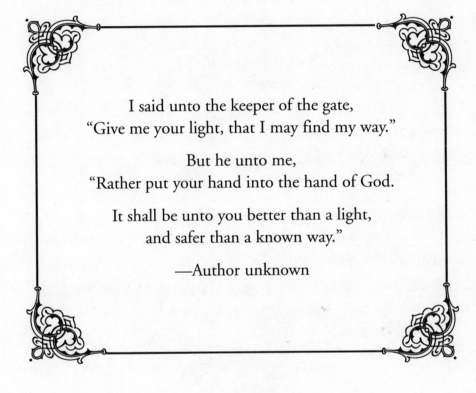

I said unto the keeper of the gate,
"Give me your light, that I may find my way."

But he unto me,
"Rather put your hand into the hand of God.

It shall be unto you better than a light,
and safer than a known way."

—Author unknown

✛ CONTACT INFORMATION ✛

If you have questions, comments, or would like to be placed on our mailing list, please contact us. We can be reached at:

Divine Line Enterprises
P.O. Box 15177
Phoenix, AZ 85060-5177
FAX (602) 977-2708

or by e-mail at:
divinelineentprs@aol.com
romaynedekanter@aol.com
evebarbieri@aol.com

To order any of our publications, please cut out and mail or fax the order form on the facing page with your payment or credit card information.

Eve Barbieri and Romayne de Kanter

If you would like to contact Sara Lyara Estes regarding your own book or Web site project, she may be reached at:

Celestial Cooperatives
P.O. Box 2231
Oroville, WA 98844-2231
(509) 476-9366 / fax (509) 476-4989
e-mail: celestia@celestcom.com

✣ ORDER FORM ✣

To order more copies of this book, send $16.95 for each copy + shipping ($3.00 for 1st copy + 50¢ for each add'l copy).

Special Offer!
SAVE 25% on 5 or more books—only $12.71 each + shipping.

ALSO AVAILABLE: GUIDED MEDITATION TAPES!
$11.00 each, including shipping (indicate quantity):

___ *Celestial White Light Protection* and a message from Archangel Michael

___ *Meeting Your Angel* and a message from Mother Mary

___ *Healing the Seven Energy Centers* and a message from Jesus

Make checks payable to Divine Line Enterprises and send to:

DIVINE LINE ENTERPRISES
P.O. Box 15177
Phoenix, AZ 85060-5177
Phone (602) 808-0324   Fax (602) 977-2708

Ship to (please print clearly):

Name _____

Address _____

City/State/ZIP _____

Phone (   ) _____ e-mail _____
___ Check/MO
___ Visa/MC#_____ - _____ - _____ - _____ Exp. Date _____

_____
Signature (cardholder)